THE SECRET TO BIG SALES

Use Executive Language to Close More Deals

Tom Searcy

with Carajane Moore

© 2023 Carajane Moore and Tom Searcy

All rights reserved.

This book or any portion thereof may not be reproduced or used in any manner whatsoever without the express written permission of the publisher except for the use of brief quotations in a book review.

Produced by Raab & Co. | Raabandco.com

RAAB&Co

Cover Design and Book Layout by Andrew Bell

Printed in the United States of America

First Publishing 2023

ISBN: 9798378457809

Blue Water Publishing
9800 Crosspoint Blvd, Suite 200
Indianapolis, IN 46256

For Tim.

Contents

	Foreword	7
	Introduction: The Language of Big Sales	10
1	Money Talks	20
2	The Authority Arc	40
3	The Fearbreakers	58
4	Your Senior Executive Buyer	74
5	The Leadership Layer Cake	92
6	Storytelling for Big Sales	108
7	Great Question!	122
	Conclusion	140
	Acknowledgments	144

Foreword

I have used and implemented the Hunt Big Sales processes and systems to explosively grow multiple organizations over the years. In particular, there is a phrase of Tom's that has always resonated with me: "You get sent to who you sound like."

In addition to being president of Terakeet, where I lead the SEO business and focus on driving top-line growth, I have founded nine companies and served as a three-time CEO. I have learned that if I am talking to a business development person about what they do and how they can help me, I decide quickly to either delegate them to someone else or ask to talk to someone higher in their company. I rarely keep engaged with the business development person unless I recognize that person has expertise in my business and my needs. They must have the insight and understanding I need from them. Otherwise, I do not want to talk to them. Period.

Often, I am on the other side of the desk, and I am selling. The Fortune 100 companies that my company works with expect me in the room. I always start with a question when I am in the position of selling to a C-suite executive. It sounds something like, "You are at 2.5% of market share in the xxxx industry. That will shrink over the next two years unless you do something different. What are you doing to not shrink, but to grow market share?" It's a question based on the contact's industry, their challenge, and their strategic approach. C-suite people have these challenges. They want to talk about these levels of issues. Everything else can be handled by someone at a lower level in their company.

MBAs are often taught a different way to consider a business and its structure as a part of their education. This helps a great deal in conversations with a senior executive. However, an MBA is not needed to speak the executive's language, get their attention, and secure their engagement. You do not even need a college degree or extensive business background. Instead, it is the language you use when framing your issues that confirms your relevance at an executive level. It is about your understanding, your questions, and your relevant responses. That's it.

This is one of the first books I have read addressing the clarity of language for "speaking executive buyer." Lots of selling books focus on the language of transactional buyers, sometimes middle-level buyers. C-suite and other executive buyers are different. Their problems are different, and they need expertise and insights. They do not care about the price of more widgets. If you want to have C-suite conversations, you must sound like them. Searcy and Moore have cracked that code. What I appreciate is that their approach is not about jargon or post-graduate language. They have written this book so that learning and speaking the language for C-suite sales calls is natural to business development people of almost any level of experience.

As a C-suite buyer, I am going to be transparent and tell you I don't particularly like spending time with salespeople. I like experts. I like people who can get my company one step further toward our goals. If a salesperson shows up at my door, by referral or because someone in my company brought them, I need to know right away if I am wasting my time. It's not hard for me to figure out.

– Mark Kennedy

INTRODUCTION

The Language of Big Sales

Very early in my career, I was in a sales meeting with my boss, the CEO of a top-five bank, and a few of the CEO's associates. Our company was worth $20 million and theirs was worth over $20 billion. My boss didn't have a presentation, and he didn't have a scripted pitch.

At that time—when I was twenty-two years old—sales training was different. A great deal of emphasis was placed on emotional and personal connections. "Friends buy from friends, so become friends with the buyer," was the belief set. It wasn't wrong. However, it didn't really apply to senior executives and C-suite buyers, who are less interested in new friends and more interested in solving specific problems. The truth is, if you want to land big sales—meaning sales that are five to ten times as large as your average sale—you have to stop trying to be a good salesperson, and instead transform yourself into a trusted expert whom your prospects have true confidence in.

It was on this call with the bank that I learned the difference between the big pitch and the language of big sales. After some pleasantries, the call went something like this:

My boss: You have a big problem, I know what it is, and if we fix it, it will be $100 million in added margin to your bank over the next three quarters if we start today. I believe we are in this meeting because you are intrigued about how to achieve this $100 million growth.

Prospect: Yeah, it would be nice, but revenue is easy, margin is harder. What can you do?

My boss: Your database is under-leveraged. More than 3% of your customer base can immediately benefit from an additional program purchase. However, if the database is better analyzed, that number is more like 15%. We will contact the highest-interest customers and offer them an add-on product, billed to your bank credit card, that will help them with shopping and discounts to the degree of a 25% reduction in cost for them. You need better management and better scripting.

Prospect: We are very protective of our customers. I cannot afford to lose any of them just to add some incremental margin. How are you going to make certain I keep every customer at the same time we do this program?

My boss: Look, you're leaking customers from your base right now. It was just published in the *Journal* that you're losing them at an annual 4% rate. As it stands right now, your customers who hold credit cards are looking for additional benefits from their credit card providers besides just the benefits of having a card and a credit line. This is a customer benefit and a brand benefit. The program creates a 2% turnover; however, the lack of a program like ours contributes to your 4%.

Prospect: I can't turn the customer base over to you and have you run at this, even though it sounds good.

My boss: Of course not. I need a sample of 200,000 customers that we will model down to a pilot for 50,000 customers. That's a fraction of a fraction of your current customers. Your team sits on top of the program to make certain it is going well, and you can pull out at any time.

Prospect: What's it cost? We'll have to run this by my CFO.

My boss: To you, it's just revenue. We work together and I will send you checks. $20 for each participating customer. The math is easy: 50,000 customers, 7,500 participants, $20/each. That's a $150,000 test contribution. For your customers, we offer a 100% guarantee.

Prospect: I'll okay this test. Work with my head of customer service and my CFO to get this done.

My boss: Excellent. Thank you. My experience has been that if you are involved in the early steps of the program start-up, the program will move more quickly. I'd like you on the first conference call.

Prospect: Okay, let's set it up.

My head was spinning a bit. There was no jargon. There was no big PowerPoint presentation. It was straightforward. But for selling to a $20 billion buyer, it felt almost too simple to me. At one point my boss slid over a couple of pieces of paper with the calculations, but that was it. As I look back at this conversation, I can see now why my boss was so effective.

1. He always talked about the bank and its customers.
2. He knew about the market and the bank's credit card competitors.
3. He knew the math and how the money worked.
4. He talked in very short statements.
5. There was more conversation than presentation.
6. The final ask was not for money, but for access to customers and teammates.

These lessons have served me well for decades and have formed the basis for this book and the insight I'm going to share with you. What was especially clear to me that day was that you don't need an MBA or PhD to master the language of big sales. To sell to executives successfully, you've got to be clear, specific, authentic, knowledgeable, and insightful. My boss only had a two-year community college degree, but it didn't matter because the way he spoke checked all those boxes.

Throw out everything you know about sales. When it comes to big sales, it's all about how you use language, and how deep you're willing to go into your prospect's world. The fact is, if you go deep enough into your prospect's world, you'll come out speaking their language and they'll have to choose you.

WHO ARE WE?

By the age of forty, I had led four corporations, growing each of them from revenues of less than $10 million to greater than $100 million, and in the last case from start-up to greater than $200 million; each in less than four years. This growth was organic, and achieved without buying, selling, or merging any of the four corporations. I was able to grow these companies through a large account sales system that I developed and implemented.

Since then, I founded Hunt Big Sales, a fast-growth consultancy and thought leadership organization. Since inception, we have landed more than $18 billion in new sales with 190 of the Fortune 500 companies, including 3M, Disney, Chase Bank, International Paper, AT&T, Apple, and more. In the process, I've established myself as a nationally recognized speaker and the foremost expert in large account sales. I am a regular contributor to the *Inc. Magazine* conferences, including the Inc. 500/500 Conferences, and Vistage International, the leading organization for CEO thought leadership, where I rank in the top 1% of speakers.

My other books include *How to Sell in Place: Closing Deals in the New Normal*, *Life After the Death of Selling: How to Thrive in the New Era of Sales*, and *RFPs Suck! How to Master the RFP System Once and for All to Win Big Business*. I am also co-author of *Whale Hunting: How to Land Big Sales and Transform Your Company* and *How to Close a Deal Like Warren Buffett: Lessons from the World's Greatest Dealmaker*. I have written weekly online columns for *Forbes*, CBS MoneyWatch, and Inc.com, which have a combined monthly readership of 38 million.

So, I know what the hell I'm talking about.

Furthermore, my sister, co-writer, colleague, and president of Hunt Big Sales, Carajane Moore, knows what she's talking about too. She was integral in landing that aforementioned $18 billion in sales, and paved new ground using the "hunt" approach in industries such as medical devices, telecommunications, technology, real estate, aviation, and construction.

Her varied experiences as a fast-track person in the sales environment have included direct sales, sales training, sales management, team sales, outside and inside sales, and entrepreneurial sales at the $10 million–plus level. Carajane has taught the Hunt Big Sales System to other professionals and consulted with major companies as a trusted advisor. She also served as a judge for the 2012 Stevie Awards and earned a degree in business administration, with an emphasis on marketing, at the University of Nebraska Omaha. Recently, Carajane was recognized as a leading woman in business and was featured in *O, The Oprah Magazine*, *Entrepreneur*, *Fortune*, and *Forbes* magazines.

WHO IS THIS BOOK FOR?

This book is for sales professionals and sales executives who are ready to land big sales. Whether you read it on your next plane ride to a meeting or buy a whole box for your team, we've landed billions in sales using the insight in this book and we want to help you do the same.

If you're tired of newfangled methodologies, apps, and analytics, you'll be pleased to know our goal is to offer straightforward, practical, and applicable advice that any sales professional could use. If you like what you read, we also offer online learning here: TheSecretToBigSales.com.

"This book is for sales professionals and sales executives who are ready to land big sales"

WHY THIS BOOK?

The US Bureau of Labor Statistics predicts there will be 22% fewer employees in sales positions by the end of 2027 than there are now. Sales activities are being transferred, downsized, and digitized. Positions that were once filled by sales professionals are being eliminated in almost every category of sales, except for one: large sales of non-commodities. Or, as I call them, big sales. This sales role is actually expected to increase in employees by 10% over the same period. This means that compensation will be going up for those sales professionals who can sell at the highest level of executive buyers. That's why this book exists. We are going to help you land big sales.

Simply being excited about your product and knowledgeable about its implementation is not enough at this level of sales. You've got to know your prospect's industry, business, and concerns at a very deep level, and you've got to truly see the world through their eyes to land the sale. In short, you've got to speak their language, and this book is your dictionary.

Big sales are made up of words—a series of successful or unsuccessful conversations. Many of us were taught to use selling words to assert our confidence, but that doesn't work at a certain level. Listening to the words your prospect uses can tell you if you're talking to the right person. Furthermore, if you identify the right person (see Chapter 4) and they are having you talk to someone else instead, you can be sure you're using the wrong words.

Using the language of big sales is about how to avoid selling. If you are selling, you will not land big sales. Instead, be solving. When you are speaking the language of the big sale, your role is to be efficient and knowledgeable, not merely confident about your solution.

Senior executive buyers talk about market share, technology, talent, legislation, regulation, competition, reputation, obsolescence, and industry life cycles. Lower-level buyers, such as those in procurement and purchasing, talk about cost, speed, and other small potatoes.

It is our goal with this book to teach salespeople how to understand words at a deeper level to navigate the sales process successfully and land bigger deals.

HOW DOES THIS BOOK WORK?

The Secret to Big Sales features personal examples from my career, example scripts for talking to clients, detailed glossaries explaining how and when to use specific terms, organizational charts and the different language you need to use at each level, and a variety of tips that will help you on your way to landing big sales. Much like learning a foreign language, immersion is the best way. Once you understand the ins and outs of translating sale speak into expert speak, you'll be able to immerse yourself in your prospect's world and come out fluent in their language. If it's getting too complex for you or your team to manage, you can always get in touch with us for further assistance at HuntBigSales.com. Below, I'll run you through what you can expect each chapter to cover:

In Chapter 1 we discuss high-level terms such as cost of goods sold (COGS) and profit and loss. You may think you know these terms, but at the executive level, they mean different things to everyone, so we need to explore how and when to use them.

In Chapter 2 we explore the Authority Arc, a helpful schema I use to make sure that my language is serving my end goal of transforming me from a mere sales professional into a trusted expert. This schema works with any existing sales process and can be repeated multiple times over the course of a deal.

In Chapter 3 I introduce fearbreakers, a set of language-based tools you can use in combination to preempt and dissolve your prospect's fears. This includes how to identify the most common fears on the buyer's team.

In Chapter 4, we explore how to identify your senior executive buyer and secure their explicit support by making specific requests.

In Chapter 5 we take a trip through the Leadership Layer Cake and analyze the needs and concerns of people at different organizational levels. This informs what language you should and should not use when selling to them.

In Chapter 6 we dissect a good sales story and give advice on how to build your own story that lands big sales.

Finally, in Chapter 7 we review numerous examples of great questions and how to ensure that the questions you ask get you the information you actually need to land the sale.

All in all, the chapters of this book piece together to breathe new life into the language you use. You've got to truly see the world through your prospect's eyes. And not just that, you've got to know the difference between how each position on the buyer's team perceives their problem and their ideal solution, and you've got to tailor your conversations to each person.

Momma always told you to watch your mouth, but she never realized you could land billion-dollar deals if you did it well enough.

CHAPTER

1

Money Talks

Every executive buyer uses financial terms differently. Know how to spot the differences.

Early in my career, I lived in apprehension of speaking to a CFO, director of finance, or whichever financial decision-making executive would be involved in completing the sale. I saw them as negative, skeptical, and close-minded. Over time, I figured out the issue: they didn't want to talk about my offering, they wanted to talk about the money. Money is the language that executives speak. They didn't want to talk about how great our solution was, how experienced our team was, or how relevant and impressive our case studies were—they wanted to talk about money. How much money in? How much money out? When will the money come in? When will the money go out? They may ask about how you do it and who you have done it for in the past, but they will only really engage in those questions once they know that the money makes sense.

You're not selling a solution, you're selling money. Money numbers are numbers that both the senior executive buyer *and* the CFO understand because money is how their success is measured.

We have been led to believe that all financial terms mean the same thing and that all reports of the same name contain the same information. This is not true. Senior leadership discusses money differently than the rest of us. Understanding how different people use different terms gives you a real leg up because you know what executive buyers mean when they talk about money.

Executives talk differently about money because they are measuring their financial position differently and for a different audience than people in sales. Just because we're all speaking in dollars and cents doesn't mean the language around those dollars and cents syncs up. While every executive position learns to speak using different money jargon, there are some common terms and usages that will be helpful to you.

"We have been led to believe that all financial terms mean the same thing and that all reports of the same name contain the same information. This is not true"

Understanding the terms has the added value of equipping you with relevant questions, which will lead to deeper and more productive conversations. If you're selling big, then your sales will impact the ways in which money is counted and valued throughout the companies you're selling to.

> ### 🧮 Napkin Math
>
> If you need a litmus test for whether or not you're prepared to talk in your buyer's language, look no further than napkin math. One of the fastest and clearest ways to demonstrate your relevance and credibility in a conversation with anyone on the buyer's team, and especially the senior executive buyer, is to calculate math with them or in front of them about their business. If you show casual expertise in the way you calculate their business and financial concerns, you will immediately impress them and be seen as a collaborator rather than a salesperson (see the Authority Arc in Chapter 2).
>
> When speaking to the prospect you could say something like the following:
>
> "Based upon your position in the marketplace and general available information, your EBITDA is probably in the range of 7% to 14%. Can we use 10% as a working number for the sake of this conversation? COGS are probably relatively light because you make chips rather

than ball bearings. For the sake of a number, let's use 10% to 20%. Generally speaking, that is a working number. You are highly automated, so you are capital intensive and labor light. Let's put the servicing of the capital at 15% and labor at 10%. I'm assuming that those are way off–can you give me some better, more workable numbers? I have about 60% tops here and you are either making amazing profits or there are more costs. Let's see, transportation is at least 10%. What am I missing?"

Napkin math draws out an enormous amount of information, even when your starting assumptions are wrong. Piece by piece, estimate by estimate, correction by correction, you wind up with a fairly clear understanding of the financial drivers of the business while also impressing your buyer.

Napkin math is just one of the important tools you'll need to understand what the prospect's concerns and contingencies are; otherwise, you won't be fully aware of what you're selling them.

THE JARGON

Most of the jargon we're going to review falls under the umbrella of Generally Accepted Accounting Practices, or GAAP. The word "Generally" is the most important part of this. All accounting practices are not the same. A strongly shared set of principles are adhered to for the reporting requirements of a bank or financial institution, a board of directors, and the IRS. However, when reviewing these terms, remember that CFOs interpret them all a little differently.

If your competitors are all using the same language in the same way, the deal is just a vendor-swap where the prospect ends up choosing a vendor based solely upon price or some random reason. This happens in big sales because the language of product, service, quality, and price are often the only topics brought to the table. In turn, the decision seems like just a comparison of these categories, and therefore doesn't require a senior executive buyer's attention at all because procurement can handle the evaluation.

Instead, to enlist the senior executive buyer, the necessary language must be relevant to their bigger challenges. This means the language must focus on time, money, and risk. For the success of this higher-level interaction, you need to use language the buyer uses: their market, competitors, industry changes, regulations, margin compression, to name a few. That language is focused on their business challenges, the real money, and what those executives see as their problems looking outward, rather than inward, where procurement looks.

The more you correctly use your prospect's language, the more credibility you will have and the more you will be seen as an equal or an expert. Read more about this in Chapter 2. Below, you'll find a list of common terms you'll need to use, their generally accepted definitions, and nuances you should watch out for when using them. Often, your buyer's team will use jargon to test your knowledge; at other times, they will use it for efficiency of communication. Either way, it's important that you understand the specific way in which your buyer is using these terms since they vary from person to person and industry to industry. There are three things you can do when you come across a new term or a term you suspect is being used differently:

1. Call It Out:
"I've heard that term used in other contexts. What does it mean here?"

2. Divert:
"Can you say what you just said in different words? I want to make certain I have it right in my notes."

3. Shoot Straight:
"I need your help. I do not know what that term/acronym means."

Even if many of the terms that follow are familiar to you, they can and often do have two or more meanings. Review them not just for your own understanding, but to ensure you are prepared when and if a prospect uses them differently from you.

Balance Sheet

🛈 Generally Accepted Definition: a statement of financial condition at a given point in time

The balance sheet is the statement of the assets, liabilities, and capital of a business at a point in time. The balance sheet, and therefore how the term is used, changes depending on how you want to represent your company. Does your product constitute an asset purchase, such as a building or a tractor? Or maybe you have an expense that is not an asset and requires depreciation? Many of the SaaS (Software as a Service) offerings in the marketplace can be represented in the income statement rather than the balance sheet. Why does that matter? Well, companies desire flexible expenses that are perceived to rise and fall based upon revenues. It is often seen by buyers as a positive if what you sell shows up in the income statement rather than the balance sheet.

Example: I never used to talk about balance sheets when selling to companies. The truth is I didn't really understand what they were in relation to the business I was selling to and the product or service I was selling. At some point, a buyer challenged me and said, "If you move this purchase from my balance sheet into my income statement, then we can do business."

"What the hell?" I said to myself. The buyer wanted to move what might show up as a depreciating asset into an operating expense. Buyers are often more interested in what report a purchase shows up on rather than the price itself. Balance sheet decisions require a different sign-off chain, often including people who do not understand your value proposition. For instance, for a computer server company, they could move their hardware from a buyer's balance sheet to their income statement by offering it as a rental or subscription instead of a purchase.

Cash Flow

ⓘ Generally Accepted Definition: the net amount of cash moving in and out of a company

Cash flow is the schedule of when receipts will be paid in the future as compared to how expenses will be paid. Understanding the importance of cash flow is vital when you are discussing the payment cycle of your own invoices in the terms of your agreement. That's because CFOs and other people in finance departments are constantly looking at their company's cash flow. They usually ask the following questions, which you should keep in mind:

→ Do we have enough money in the "checkbook" to pay for the bills as they are coming in or will we have to draw money from our credit line?
→ Are our invoices being paid in full and on a timely basis as contractually agreed?

Finance people want to pay their bills as late as possible and receive their checks for invoices as soon as possible. In my experience, cash flow typically shows up in the "Terms" part of a contract or agreement. Companies are concerned about how the fees or purchases from your company will fit into their cash flow.

> **Example:** I was once involved in an eight-figure sale with a midsize company selling to a Fortune 500 company. The division we were selling into—which claimed billions of dollars in revenue—was pressing us for difficult pricing. Through our discussions, we determined that they did not actually have a pricing problem, they had a cash flow problem. They were held at the division level to a certain size of purchase as it impacted projected cash flow. We changed the terms and payment schedule to meet their cash flow requirements and did not have to change the price.

"**The more you correctly use your prospect's language, the more credibility you will have and the more you will be seen as an equal or an expert**"

Cost of Goods Sold (COGS)

🛈 Generally Accepted Definition: the total cost to produce a given company's goods, including labor and materials

What are all the costs of making a product? This includes raw materials, labor, and suppliers of additional services on a unit-by-unit basis. COGS is the arbitrarily defined list and assigned amounts of money that it takes a company to create what they sell, as closely defined down to a unit or a unique customer as possible. Like many financial words, it suggests that this term is used by all companies in the same way. It. Is. Not.

Companies that might make the same product attribute components of their COGS differently so it's important to understand how your buyer's organization defines its COGS.

A buyer might tell you, "We are trying to reduce our COGS by such-and-such amount every year for the next three years. Can you help with this?" This is a dream question. If you look at each component of the COGS, you now have an opportunity to determine your reduction rate. It doesn't have to equal all of the amount, but you know what amount you are selling to achieve.

> **Example:** There was a company that manufactured tractors that were both expensive to produce and expensive for the farmers. The company wanted to reduce the cost it took to make the tractors so they could make more margin and also reduce prices if needed. What the selling company did was to show that not only were some of their gauges less expensive, but their gauges were also easier to install. Installation efforts and price per unit reduced the COGS for the tractor maker.

Cost of Sale (COS)

ⓘ **Generally Accepted Definition:** the total cost for a given company to sell the goods it makes

This term usually refers to the cost of adding a new customer. It includes many sales-related expenses in one number: advertising, marketing, digital marketing, commissions, travel, entertainment, CRM systems, and so on. Obviously most people want to keep this number as low as possible. If you hear your buyer say something like, "We are cutting our budget on marketing by half this year," then you've got to ask what their current COS is.

Marketing is typically measured as a part of the cost of sale. Find out if there is a new targeted COS—what services, conferences, digital expenditures, channel partners, and so on are going to be the way in which the prospect executive will be selling? Using the language of cost of sale opens the conversation to secure more complete information. It also demonstrates that you understand how expenses are measured for the senior executive buyer.

> **Example:** There was a digital marketing company that sold their benefits the way many in the industry do–in terms of "market reach," "number of views," "length of time on site," and "number of visits to site." These are great numbers for a digital marketer to benchmark their own performance on, but they are not exactly helpful for the businesses that hire them. Companies don't just want more people brought to their doorstep–that's more work for them and their own sales team. What would be more helpful is if a marketing firm promised to lower a company's COS in meaningful and reportable ways via digital marketing. That is an example of speaking in your customer's language rather than expecting them to understand yours.

👉 Who the hell are *you*?

As we'll see more specifically in Chapter 2, my goal in this book is to help you go from a professional salesperson to a trusted expert. The way you use words is key to this transformation. The way you talk and the words you use must show your senior executive buyer that you're not only passionate about their business but you're also an expert in their industry who can see the world through their lens. There are four vital questions you should ask yourself on your journey to understanding: Who are you to them? Why are they using the words they use? Where is their attention? And what difference are you going to make?

1. Who are you to them?

It's important that senior executives know that you understand their world; they aren't there to mentor you or teach you their business. There is an old saying, "Intelligence makes statements. Wisdom asks questions." An expert asks different questions because the expert understands the language of the senior executive buyer. You could ask, "What do you mean?" when you hear a term you don't understand, or you could ask, "How do you calculate that at your company?" One question shows ignorance, the other shows expertise. See Chapter 7 for more questions to keep in your back pocket.

2. Why are they using the words they use?

You've got to understand the "why" behind the terms that are being thrown around. Why do CFOs always talk about the EBIDTA while purchasing department executives always talk about gross margin? Senior executive buyers are giving you clues as to the macro impact that will cause them to make a purchase. As we'll talk about later in this book, each layer of management and leadership in a buying company has its own priorities, perspectives, and measures for what is considered success. At the senior level, those motivations are different and use different language, and if you don't use and understand those terms, you will miss the clues tipping you off to the motivations.

3. Where is their attention?

Everyone answers to someone else. Even owners must please the bankers and the IRS. Whether it is a senior executive in a company, someone lower, or someone in the chief experience officer role, that person's performance is measured by a number on a report. For the highest-level buyers of a big sale, those numbers are on the financial reports. Knowing the terms means that you know the report and the goal that the buyer is trying to achieve.

4. What difference are you going to make?

What difference does your difference make? Big sales are about moving the big needles of money in a company. If what you are selling does not move a big needle on the financial dashboard of the senior executive buyer, then you will neither interest nor meaningfully engage that buyer.

EBITDA

ⓘ Generally Accepted Definition: earnings before interest, taxes, depreciation, and amortization

Many companies use EBITDA as a financial measure of success. It's so important that they base their revenue targets, operating budgets, bonuses, and other important line items on it. It represents the gross earnings you're left with (i.e., profit) after you subtract interest paid on current debt, taxes you expect to pay on profits, the calculated losses certain assets will experience, and the amortization of the cost on assets over time. Add to your understanding of this concept the additional trend of companies being evaluated by using a multiplication of the EBITDA by some factor to determine what a purchase price should be. This added use explains why there is so much interest in it.

What does it really mean? Well, companies are looking for ways to increase this valuation to benefit either management, shareholders, or purchasers. The senior leadership, CEO, and owners are looking at this one number as a measurement of the company's success. They want to know how working with you will improve their short-term and long-term EBITDA. How will your sale help them achieve that goal?

We have worked with many companies seeking to sell their businesses within eighteen months. For those companies, EBITDA was very important because their sale price would be calculated as a multiple of EBITDA. For these companies, there would always be a question of price. And we'd always answer, "It's free." We would explain that our services would increase their multiple by one or two. This means that companies calculating their sales price as six times would now sell their company for seven or eight times the EBITDA. Our fees were such a small number compared to the multiple that the conversation moved quickly away from concerns about price.

Warren Buffett and Charlie Munger of Berkshire Hathaway refer to EBITDA as "la-la land." It's a land where companies hide bad decisions and mask the intrinsic value of their businesses. Regardless, Wall Street likes it and sometimes confuses it with actual value. When I work with companies where I can talk to the owner, often EBITDA doesn't come up in conversations unless they are preparing for a sale. The owner wants to know, "How much money am I going to make and how much will buying what you are selling impact that?" The owner is looking all the way to the bottom of the lines of a financial report and wants to know how much value the business has. It's a great selling offset to EBITDA when talking with owners.

"If what you are selling does not move a big needle on the financial dashboard of the senior executive buyer, then you will neither interest nor meaningfully engage that buyer"

> **Example:** A company that did medical sample testing for a variety of hospitals was approached by a competitor to be purchased. The testing company was being valued as a multiple of their average three-year EBITDA. The testing company being bought wanted the highest price it could get, so it focused on not only the historical EBITDA but the fact that it was expected to increase over the next several years. A strong sales generation system added to the final purchase price from a traditional six-times EBITDA to seven-and-a-half-times EBITDA, a 20% improvement simply by boosting EBITDA.

General and Administrative Costs

ⓘ Generally Accepted Definition: the total operating expenses to run a business

General and administrative costs (also known as "the G and A") are the static costs of running a business. This usually includes rent, utilities, office staff, office supplies, and so on. If what you are selling increases or decreases the G and A, that expense that is static now changes. Companies do not like to increase their G and A without a corresponding increase in revenue, or gross margin. G and A is seen as "the price of doing business." Finance people want to keep this amount stable and not increasing.

A buyer might tell you, "We have a policy of zero net change during a fiscal year in our overall G and A." As a salesperson, you are being told that anything that you sell into the company that affects general and administrative costs must deliver at least the same amount of benefit as the expense.

> **Example:** A company was frustrated by the high cost of their office supplies expense across all of its national locations. Paper, pens, staples, and more were being purchased at inconsistent prices and volumes. All of these supplies came under the heading of general and administrative costs. Through the use of a supplies inventory and forecasting system, overall G and A costs were reduced.

Gross Margin (GM)

ⓘ Generally Accepted Definition: the amount of money remaining after the cost of producing goods is subtracted from the revenue earned from their sale

If you subtract the cost of goods sold from the revenue, you get the gross margin. The GM typically shows up as both a dollar amount and a percentage. What's important for you to remember is that if what you provide impacts the manufacture or creation of a product or service, it will occur "above the line." That means that you are helping improve the GM of a company by increasing revenue without increasing the costs of manufacturing or serving individual customers.

Likewise, if you can show that you will reduce the COGS for those items, you will be making yourself very valuable.

While CFOs are usually looking at EBITDA, gross margin is often the playground of the purchasing department, which only understands the word "less." Generally, they are looking for a lower price on the components needed to make a product or provide a service. Unless you can creatively show how you will cut costs or increase revenue, you will have a tough time selling.

Example: An automobile manufacturer's purchasing department was under constant pressure to reduce costs so that the company's cars would be competitively priced. Knowing that the gross margin would be all that the purchasing department cared about, they designed a new strategy. The costs per unit for their own product would stay the same, a bit more than the current competitor, but the man-hours for training and being part of the production line would be lower. This was a net reduction in the overall expense of making the car that didn't require the company to drop its own price.

Profit and Loss
ℹ️ **Generally Accepted Definition:** a statement summarizing a business's revenue, profit, and losses

The profit and loss (P/L) report answers the question: is the company actually making money? This is a standard category of report for every company, but not necessarily the same report for each. Some companies use it as a measure of the performance of their business when compared to projections. Some companies use it as a forecasting tool. Frequently in sales calls and presentations, a member of the buying team will ask about how purchasing from you will impact their P/L. The P/L also includes the net margin, which is what most of us call profit. It's shown as revenue minus COGS, COS, and G and A from the revenue.

Often, the language I have heard has been, "When will this hit our P and L?" The question reflects when the customer will have to explain the purchase as it relates to the profit at a particular point in time. Often, P/L measured over a year will normalize out their purchase. The amount paid is spread out over the twelve months. However, when it is an all-in purchase, such as a piece of machinery or technology, the question is about during which month or quarter the P/L will reflect the purchase.

Shrinkage
ℹ️ **Generally Accepted Definition:** the amount of inventory lost due to theft, damage, fraud, or error

This is the amount of manufactured inventory that is made but not delivered to the customer nor paid for. Typical causes of shrinkage include internal theft, damage in warehouse, damage in transportation, and lost goods. Companies perform regular inventories to control for items being lost, stolen, or simply unused.

Example: If you have ever spent a night in a hospital, you may be curious as to why someone comes in twice a day to scan all the equipment in the room. They use a little scanner like you see in a grocery store. They scan the bed, metal pole for the IV, the chair, and so on. Why? Do they think someone has stolen the bed in the night and left me behind? No. It's because they want to know where all their expenses are and how their equipment is being used, and to document its use to charge the insurance company. If the hospital can't find or didn't use a piece of equipment, it would be attributed to shrinkage.

Three Buzzwords You Should Know

Sometimes, the use of certain financial buzzwords serves as a subtle show of whether or not you are experienced enough to be a good provider. Three of the most common are below.

1. Accretive

I must say, this is the stupidest and most overused CEO word of the 2020s. There must have been a book put out or a TED talk that used this word, because it is used as regularly as "the." It supposedly makes people sound smart, but it simply means that there is an increase from one number to another number. Companies are looking for revenue that is "accretive." This term is often used to describe the type of customers or revenues to be added over time. This could be in relation to a product line, market, or new acquisition. Regardless, it is used most often to mean "increase," "additional," or "improvement."

2. Velocity

Everyone uses the term "velocity." In the business environment when you are either buying or selling, the measure of velocity is one of the throughputs. It can be relevant to the capacity of a system. When the velocity can be increased, it increases the total capacity of that system. This could be a technical system, marketing system, manufacturing system. If your work with a company provides an improvement in the velocity of part of a system, you have increased the capacity of the overall system. A grocery store representative might use the term to describe the frequency at which a particular product is bought or sold.

> **3. Yield**
> In agriculture, we hear about the yield of a crop from an acre of field during a given season. It's as simple as how much input will produce how much output. In nonagricultural terms, companies are looking to diminish waste and unnecessary material handling and increase output. Even in SaaS systems, yield shows up as a measure because of the amount of work and training required to provide the highest output

Now that you understand all of these terms, it's important to remember that their definitions are constantly changing. That is, there is a range of definitions for each term. You have got to focus on understanding your buyer and letting them know you understand the nuances of their point of view.

I once watched a debate between two of the smartest and most articulate pundits of the time, William F. Buckley and George Will. Buckley was famous for his vocabulary and complex ideas. At one point in the debate, Buckley teased Will. He said, "George, you are keeping up with all of this, I hope. You seem rather simple in your answers." To which Will replied, "William, you speak to be *heard* by a very few, whereas I speak to be *understood* by everyone."

Remember, senior executive buyers are not measuring salespeople by the number of syllables in their words, they are looking for a common understanding with someone who speaks their language.

⭐ Key Takeaways

1. There is a language to big sale math that executive buyers and you need to agree on (see page 21).

2. Senior executive buyers use terms you need to know to connect with what their problems are so that you can help solve them (see page 22).

3. Senior executive buyers use financial impact represented by money terms to make decisions. The closer you come to speaking in their terms, the more successful your selling will be (see page 24).

4. Not all terms, even though standard in the market, mean the same thing to your buyer (see page 24).

5. Find more relevant resources at TheSecretToBigSales.com.

CHAPTER

2

The Authority Arc

Use language to land big sales by transforming yourself from a mere salesperson into an industry expert.

While for small sales the process is usually two-dimensional—meet → propose → meet → close—big sales require an additional dimension in order to contain the added complexity of the deals. I call this added dimension the Authority Arc, and it's helped land billions of dollars in sales. Big sales involve more stakeholders, more money, and more complexity—that means they involve more work for you. The Authority Arc is a schema that helps transform you from a sales professional into an expert authority. The entirety of the arc could be traveled over your standard sales process, or over the course of a single phone call, or both! Chances are, you'll have to repeat the Authority Arc steps at numerous times throughout the big sale process.

Senior executive buyers don't see the world the way you do, so you need to put on special goggles that help you understand the additional dimensions and complexity that big sales involve. In this chapter, I'll walk you through what the Authority Arc looks like, regardless of your sales process. If you keep the Authority Arc on your mind as you engage your senior executive buyer, I promise you'll be landing big sales in no time.

Let's take Kevin Smith, for instance—that's not his real name, but he'll probably know I'm talking about him.

Kevin is a professional salesperson. He has lots of customers, he has won lots of deals, and his customers really like him. However, he has not closed any big sales. Kevin has achieved his current success thanks to the relationships he has developed with his lower-level buyers. He follows a typical process:

1. Have a first meeting with the prospect where you explain what you do and ask some questions.
2. Send a proposal.
3. Meet again, answer questions, and ask for the client's business.
4. Have a closing meeting.
5. Do the business.
6. Meet with the customer regularly to check that they are happy and ask for more business.

While this is a good recipe for closing small sales, Kevin needs to step up his game to land the big sales. The higher you reach up a large company's organizational chart, the more your process and language need to match that level.

I once saw Kevin come back from his second meeting with a senior vice president at a Fortune 500 company. He was vibrating with excitement. And then he uttered the five most dangerous statements in sales:

> **"They friggin' love us!"** **"They want a proposal!"** **"This could be huge!"**
> **"Darn near done deal!"**
> **"This is 99% closed!"**

While it's clear he had a cordial meeting that was not a complete failure, the truth is, buyers want solutions, not friends. When a salesperson says something like, "These people love us!" I know I am about to listen to a completely meaningless tale of smiles and laughter: "We have a lot in common, same football teams, a couple of us went to the same schools. We even had some of the same professors! They heard our company had a good reputation and they hope we can do something together." Details like this are quaint but they mean close to nothing. Do not confuse motions with movement. Phone calls, emails, texts, and meetings—every CRM file is filled with the date, time, and results of these actions. The more of these in the account file, the more it looks as if there is progress being made in selling and growing the account. These are all motion. A flurry of activity with little progress.

"The Authority Arc is a schema that helps transform you from a sales professional into an expert authority"

Senior executive buyers expect a friendly business conversation. They believe that you and your people are good. They also are courteous, friendly, and funny with their customers. They know how to be charming and create a sense of camaraderie themselves. However, these interactions do not mean a decision in your favor. If you are still getting caught up in details like this, you're not seeing the whole picture. Let's put on our X-ray goggles to understand why Kevin's excitement is a bit premature:

- → No one executive ever commits to a big sale alone. There are always other people considering the proposed solution.
- → Big sales rarely close fast. There are numerous considerations and details to be ironed out. Two meetings are never enough.
- → Nothing denotes "love" like a check. While chemistry with a potential client is necessary, it does not equal a sale. That is even more true for big sales, where "buying" and "liking" are not synonymous.
- → Fast proposals mean fast delays. People who ask for a quick turnaround on a proposal are either price-shopping or want to exit the process quickly.

Big sales happen because big people have big problems and need big and fast solutions. Big sales take a lot of time, a lot of thinking, and a lot of work. If you're seeing deals in two dimensions, chances are you won't close many big sales because senior executive buyers will see that you don't grasp the whole picture and therefore cannot be trusted with their resources, time, or business.

> ### 😊 No Degree, No Problem!
>
> Mark Twain famously warned that you should "never let schooling get in the way of your education." I agree. Most true experts learned not from books, but from making mistakes and paying the cost. I will confess, I believe that the cost-benefit ratio of going to college is growing more out of proportion every day. Sure, I want my doctors, lawyers, and accountants to get a formal degree, however, learning on the job has always been more important. It provides real experience rather than leaving you to rely on bookish case studies. Your credibility as an expert salesperson comes from your stories of success and failure. Your senior executive buyer probably doesn't care what college you went to, and they definitely don't care about your GPA.

AUTHORITY ARC BEST PRACTICES

The following guidelines will ensure your success when using this schema in your sales process:

1. Do Not Skip a Step

Follow the steps of the arc in order and do not skip a step. Confirm you have an understanding and agreement with the potential buyer on that step before moving to the next step.

2. Define the Terms

When presenting your information and ideas to a prospect, make sure to explain the context for each term. This applies to each stage of the arc. If providing a market analysis, be crystal-clear as to what market, during what period, and under what conditions. Senior executive buyers resent having to dig deeper for information when you can easily provide all the details.

3. Do This Every Time

There is a mistaken belief that because you have communicated with a senior executive buyer at a given level on the Authority Arc, that this is where you can pick up the conversation or presentation. Wrong. At any subsequent meeting, you will always need to start at the beginning of the process, reviewing the data, analysis, and so on. The key is to be brief and summarize all the previous stages. This provides context for the conversation and reminds the senior executive buyer of what has been understood and agreed up until this point in the sales process.

4. Senior Executive Buyer First

This model of communication and persuasion is designed for the senior executive buyer, who leads the purchasing team in their decision-making process. The senior buyer's agreement at each step of the process ensures that the sale can move forward. If you are delegated to a level beneath the senior executive buyer, you will need to go through the entire Authority Arc again, up until the point where you left off.

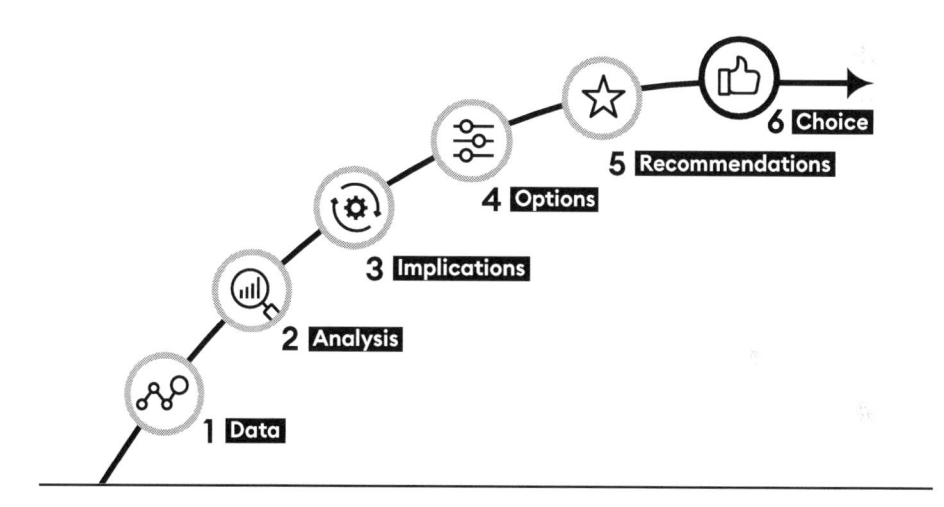

1 Data
2 Analysis
3 Implications
4 Options
5 Recommendations
6 Choice

THE AUTHORITY ARC

Each part of the Authority Arc is leveraged from the previous stage. Data is leveraged into analysis; analysis is leveraged into implications; implications are leveraged into options; options are leveraged into recommendations; and recommendations are leveraged into choices. Let's drill down into these stages one by one.

For the examples used in the Authority Arc section, we will be referring to an example from the SEO industry.

Quick definition of SEO: SEO stands for "search engine optimization." It is the process of optimizing a website or web page to improve its visibility and ranking in search engine results pages (SERPs). This can be achieved through various techniques, such as using keywords in the content and meta tags, building backlinks, and optimizing the website's structure and code. The goal of SEO is to increase organic traffic to a website by making it more visible and relevant to search engines and users.

1. Data

Agreed-upon data is the foundation for all of a deal's stages. Data declares the current state of the prospect's market, problems, and successes. Data is frequently statistical in nature. The information often comes from the prospect or from research about its industry. Data can also come from information gathered about competitors and other prospects in the marketplace.

There is often data about competition, international issues, regulation, and margin compression between last year's pricing and costs compared to this year. Many times, your company will have provided the information for your prospect's industry. There are key questions that will help you discover facts that your competitors do not know and will provide you with an advantage.

> **Example:** A large internet marketing services provider with robust SEO services wanted to solve more important SEO problems than their competitors. The data was gathered on the prospect, its industry, competitors, customers, and overall marketplace. This comprehensive data was broader in scope than the data provided by competitors and included additional categories of information.

2. Analysis

Analysis involves calculations, estimates, and projections based on agreed-upon data.

Data is usually complex while analysis is not. Analysis is how data is leveraged by salespeople. Analysis explains what the data provided means right now. In a meeting, you might say: "Your sales of this category of your parts have increased at the rate of 10% over last year. That's faster than your competitors and ranks you as third in market share." In this sentence, the data is the 10%, but it has little context or value until you add the analysis that this ranks the company in third place among competitors.

> **Example:** SEO analysis by the provider showed several things to the prospect:
>
> → It was losing its own prospects because its competitors were capturing interest that the company should have been capturing.
> → It was on a downward slide in interest share as measured by declining qualified customer interest.
> → Cost per qualified customer was increasing significantly as compared with competitors.
> → Message interest had diminished based upon time on page from qualified customers.

3. Implications

Implications are how experts leverage analysis. Implications enter us into the world of predicting the future. Salespeople sell what will solve the problems of today, but senior executive buyers are buying to solve the problems of *tomorrow*. The language of big sales is the language of understanding the now, then helping the prospect see a probable future.

→ What will the data and analysis mean over a period of time?
→ What will happen if a prospect continues to do what they are doing?
→ What is the context of achieving what they will achieve if they continue to do what they are doing?

Example: The SEO marketing company looked at the data around SEO usage and the analysis showing trends as it considered what future issues would come up for a banking customer. Paid advertising over the internet was increasing in volume of click-throughs and cost per click but was showing a lower revenue yield overall. The analysis was that SEO was diminishing in its success in attracting new customers for the bank, but further analysis indicated that other banks were having the same problem. The implication here is that the customer acquisition world was stagnant in general and its cost per click would be increasing under the current strategy. This increase would occur at a faster pace than competitors if the strategy was not changed.

4. Options

Options are how salespeople leverage their implications to explain to their prospects what the possible solutions are.

The old adage for selling was "always be closing," but for big sales, you need to always be solving. You are not expected to be a salesperson, you are expected to be an expert who can solve problems in the prospect's market, with their competitors, or as regards upcoming regulations they're going to navigate.

A senior executive buyer's role is often to deploy capital to solve problems or increase performance. They are at the poker table of business decisions looking for the sure thing. As the expert, your role is to present choices for the senior executive buyer to consider. The point is, you are the expert who has helped the senior executive buyer seek options.

Example: The SEO company can present three courses of action for the bank to use to sign up customers faster than its competitors. The SEO company should also include the pros and cons of each decision.

1. Stick with paid ad options: Yes, it had a diminishing rate of return, but it was also predictable. The pro is that you don't have to change anything, the con is you'll keep getting what you're getting.

2. Move to a new customer acquisition model: Organic search as a driving approach to gaining visibility and interest. The pro is that this route has demonstrated a lot of success in financial services, the con is that you're trying something new, and we don't know if it's what your customers want.

3. Brand and market: Change tactics and invest in branding and marketing. The pro is that your brand will definitely be more recognizable, the con is that it takes time, costs a lot of money, and only has indirect yield.

"Salespeople sell what will solve the problems of today, but senior executive buyers are buying to solve the problems of tomorrow"

5. Recommendations

Of course, you want to recommend that your prospect choose the option that involves hiring you—this is how you leverage the options.

However, you should not make your option seem so good and the others so bad that you're trapping the prospect. You are making an expert recommendation as to the best course of action selected from the options presented.

At this point in the sales process, your prospect should see you as a trusted advisor. For this reason, you can state, "Of these options, we believe that the option that we represent produces the best results." The next statements from your prospects and the buying team should be questions, challenges, or affirmations. You should have organized your conversations throughout the sales process in such a way that most of their objections and questions have been answered by this point.

Example: Move forward with option 2 for the purposes of:
→ larger as compared to current yield
→ greater reach
→ lower cost per interested and qualified customer.

---

6. Choices

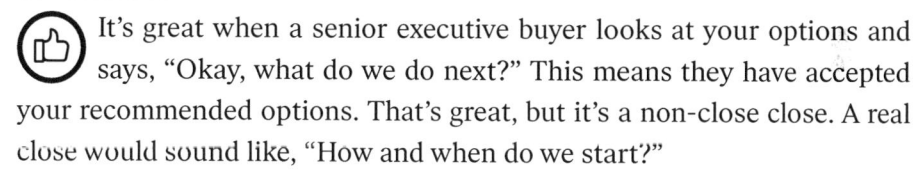

It's great when a senior executive buyer looks at your options and says, "Okay, what do we do next?" This means they have accepted your recommended options. That's great, but it's a non-close close. A real close would sound like, "How and when do we start?"

Example: To start the process of maximizing the new approach to the SEO and relevant services from the current provider, several things were required:
→ Permission to access the technical staff for implementation
→ Coordination with the marketing team
→ A switch over from the current provider to this company for a smooth handoff.

THE AUTHORITY ARC

A plan was provided with the necessary requests, resources needed including personnel, and timeline. This had to be signed off on by the senior executive buyer. The plan demonstrated that there was a how and when for starting.

Promises

Once the choice has been made, you and your prospect can set off on the road to gold. You can now leverage their choice to close the deal.

When someone asks, "What do we do next?" they are asking not just for themselves—big sales involve big teams—but for the rest of the buying team as well as related departments such as finance, technology, and others who need to be involved in the promise. The senior executive buyer will expect a detailed plan this team can follow.

Whether this promise happens during a single phone call or through a six-month sales process, in each case, they can feel in control because you are presenting information that they can review, approve, or provide adjustments to along the way. At each step they feel that they are dealing with a professional and expert. When they provide information—possibly confidential information—they will know that they are doing it for a particular reason that benefits them.

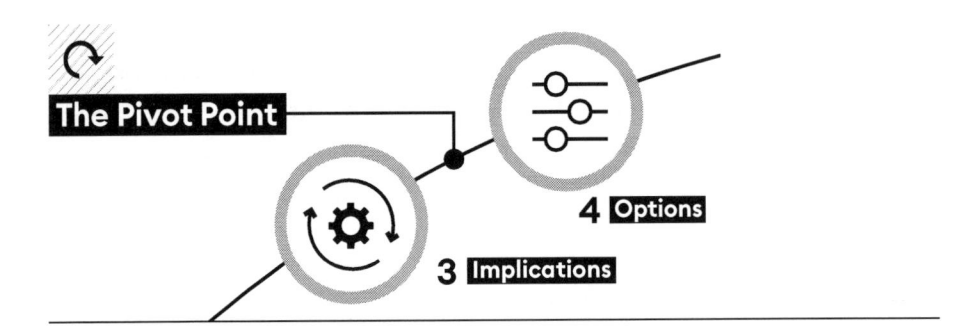

The Pivot Point

4 Options

3 Implications

THE PIVOT POINT

The higher we move along the Arc, the more trust you have built with your senior executive buyer based on your demonstrated insight and expertise. The pivot point is when you shift from a sales professional to an expert authority. The early steps can be achieved mostly through research and education, but the influence of these endeavors diminishes the further along in the process you go. Merely being educated and well-researched does not provide the insight, expertise, or mastery you need to land a big sale. As we take the senior executive buyer through the Authority Arc, what is most valued is that the future can be predicted starting at the implications stage.

It is common for even the savviest executive to become singularly focused. Whether it be issues in the business, pressure from the board, information from the most recent conference—all of these can grab the attention of a senior executive buyer and hold it. However, if you only know what everyone else knows, you have no advantage and you are not an expert, you're just keeping up with the common knowledge of your industry.

Being an expert on your senior executive buyer's industry, challenges, and future requires a deep dive. Doing Google searches, reading trade blogs, and listening to industry-relevant podcasts are all great and appropriate. But what can you do beyond that? I believe in being well informed on everything going on in the area and marketplace of your prospect's world.

In one instance, a company manufacturing solvents and lubricants was in the top five by revenue rankings for competitors in their industry. In conversations with the senior executive buyer, expertise was shown through a discussion of new regulations. The regulations did not affect any of the ingredients used in their products but had to do instead with intra-country reduced quotas. The expert statement was not about products but about policy. That is the difference between looking at only the industry and therefore missing the expert viewpoint that will land you the deal. These deep dives are the price of admission to the land of big sales. As your company demonstrates a greater vision of the future, which is what an expert does, it will be seen as a partner that understands the buyer's company and its challenges.

COMMON MISTAKES

It might take some time for you to get your sea legs with the Authority Arc. With practice, it will become second nature, whether over the course of a phone call or a whole sales cycle, for you to constantly be proving yourself as an expert. There are still four main mistakes I see when people use the Authority Arc:

1. Making It All About You

Many salespeople only talk about their offerings and include facts and analysis as if they were ornaments on a tree! There is a false presumption that the solution is what will make the purchase. With big sales, that is not the case. The senior executive buyer is focused on what you know about the problems the company is facing and your expert opinion. The fact that you may represent the best choice is actually the ornament on the tree. Big sales require the absolute alignment of the first stages of the Authority Arc before your solution will even seriously be considered.

2. Asking Instead of Telling

Your buyer is talking to you because they want you to solve their problems, not because they want to educate you—they don't have time for that. If you are asking your buyer, "What keeps you up at night?" or "If you could wave a magic wand, what would you change?" then your prospect will know that you haven't done your homework. It also tells them that they are just another sales call. It tells them to not waste their time. They either put you off for some time in the future or delegate you to someone at a lower level in the company. To be successful, your data and analysis need to be ready at the very first meeting. At this stage, you can find out what agreements and disagreements you have and incorporate that information into the implications stage.

3. Skipping Implications

Remember Rule #1 from the Authority Arc best practices? Don't skip a step. If you don't give the implications of the analysis, your recommendations will have no value. I have seen so many sales professionals jump from analysis straight to recommendations. They do this for several reasons. Often it is because their prospect is excited and requesting a proposal. Sometimes there is great chemistry with the prospect that makes a sales professional— like Kevin—feel as though they are on the same page and just need to get a proposal out. Sales professionals are impatient in this way. The downside is that, when it comes to big sales, the solution often looks incredibly expensive if it doesn't come with the implications and the alternative options.

"To be successful, your data and analysis need to be ready at the very first meeting"

4. Settling for Nibble Buys

"Let's start out with a smaller project and that way we can test things out and make certain we are working together well." This is a nibble buy. If this happens, you can assume one or more of six things:

1. They don't believe that the problem they have can be solved as quickly as it needs to be by your solution.
2. They do not know what the size and urgency of the problem is that you are proposing to solve.
3. Somewhere along the sales process, you did not get agreement on one of the stages.
4. You are talking to the wrong level of person.
5. You are talking about the wrong problems.
6. You went for the close before the senior executive buyer completely understood the impact of not saying yes.

The Authority Arc provides salespeople with a course of conversations and presentations that create a logical buying process for big sales. It's better to not think of this as just another sales process, but a process of understanding where you position your company as the best partner for solving your prospect's unique problems. While fancy presentations and nurturing friendships are helpful, anyone can do that, so they don't necessarily increase your chances of landing the deal. Using the Authority Arc to ensure that your language is targeted and establishes you as an expert to your buyer is a tried-and-true way to increase your chances of landing big sales.

⭐ Key Takeaways

1. The Authority Arc creates a selling conversation structure that can be used for all sales touchpoints (see page 41).

2. The Authority Arc positions the sales professional as an expert and trusted advisor (see page 43).

3. Each step of the Authority Arc must be followed in order and agreed to upon its completion by the senior executive buyer before you embark on the next step (see page 44).

4. The ideal outcome of following the Authority Arc is to establish yourself as an expert for your senior executive buyer (see page 56).

5. Find more relevant resources at TheSecretToBigSales.com.

CHAPTER

3

The Fearbreakers

Learn to identify and neutralize your buyer's fears before they ruin your deal.

Every CEO, president, and owner is constantly asking themselves two questions: What happens if we make good choices, and what happens if we make bad choices? However, as sales professionals, we often respond to these questions by telling prospects that they shouldn't worry about *anything* because our solution will take care of *everything*. Salespeople tend to set aside their prospects' fears in favor of persuading with overwhelming excitement when, in fact, it is our insight and expertise—not our mere enthusiasm—that will allay their fears. Until their fears and the risks they face are reasonably addressed, prospects will be unable to see the growth opportunities you might offer.

In most cases, your advocates on the buyer's side are working behind the scenes to diminish fears on your behalf, so you have to provide the language to help them do this. In one instance, my client was selling to a senior executive buyer within one of the top-ten insurance companies. There was a meeting between his team of eleven different department heads and our team of six. The meeting started with our senior executive buyer, Jimmy, hammering question after question in the meeting. We answered one and he would give another. All of them were delivered with a sarcastic tone of disbelief. When we answered each question, he would sit back in his chair and say, "Okay, that makes sense" or "I like that." Then he would lean forward with another hammering question. After an hour of this, our team and Jimmy stepped into a side conference room. He closed the door and said, "You guys were great! I knew none of my team would ask any real questions, so I had to push you guys to get all the answers out. I think this is going to work very well. Send me the final contract. We're going to be smoothed out now on our side." We had armed him with the language to break his team's fears on our behalf.

"It is our insight and expertise— not our mere enthusiasm— that will allay their fears"

This illustrates a tactic I like to call fearbreakers: structured answers, responses, tactics, and challenges that work to neutralize fear. Senior executive buyers and other executives on their team cannot embrace solutions until all fears are reduced. First, let's talk about where these fears often come from.

THE GENEALOGY OF EXECUTIVE FEAR

As you know by now, executives use different words, define those words differently, and see the world and your offering through a lens much different than most. While their stated goals might be to "achieve excellence," become a "market leader," or provide "flawless service," those shiny public-facing goals represent a complex amalgam of fears, risks, and potential opportunities. As a salesperson, it's your job to skillfully address the underlying complexity rather than the faux corporate speak you'll often be fed. Let's dive into the usual suspects when it comes to executive fear.

Accountability

Every member of the buyer's team has a level of concern about who gets blamed if the choice does not produce. The bigger the sale, the greater the sense of risk. There is a phrase, "Success has a thousand parents, failure is an orphan." Many will claim credit for decisions and choices that work. The senior executive buyer wants the solution you are promising, but needs a "fall guy" if it doesn't. That's a category of fear—not about whether the solution will work, but about who will get the blame if it doesn't.

Change

The ambiguous and uncertain future created by changing from what is currently being done or purchased to another choice fosters a sense of uneasiness. Members of the buyer's team have long memories of changes that caused problems or damages within the company when those changes were implemented. It is a natural condition of being a human that any change is scary and for any reason, but the degrees are different. The larger the change, the larger the fear.

Friction

Within big companies, there is an ongoing and usually courteous fight occurring between departments. Resources are finite and needs are larger than the resources. One department will get more or less than another. It's not enough for a member of the buyer's team to look at the "piece of the pie" of resources that they have. They also look at a peer's piece to see who got more pie. Companies do the same thing with initiatives that are being supported. One initiative receives more resources than another. There is a concern that if your solution is purchased, it may not be perceived well by all of the members of the buyer's team. Does buying your solution take from someone else's resources?

Work

"I'm so glad that your company is coming on board because the process will take up a lot of resources and time and that is just what I was looking for," said no buyer ever. Every change comes with effort. The greater the change, the greater the perceived effort. We all believe that, in the end, our solution is better and saves time. However, in the short term, the fear is that it will take time. IT never has enough resources and every addition to their workload is a three-alarm fire that comes with pushback. All because of the fear that buying from you may cause more work for someone inside of the buying team.

Mistakes

As with accountability, the buyer's team members are afraid of mistakes. In this category it is not about blame, it is about impact. What will a mistake caused by buying from or hiring you cause to that buyer and their work and team? Will it be money, losing face with other departments, or possibly losing credibility with senior management? Mistakes in one area of a big company are often hard to contain. Because big companies are ecosystems, every new entrant potentially can upset more than just its area of effort.

Knowing the genealogy of executive fears can help you develop strategies to address these fears so that you do not have to face them later in the buying process.

> ### ⊘ Wrong Number
>
> An example of friction from earlier in my career was working with a long-distance carrier, MCI. At the time, long-distance was a very competitive market for telephone companies and they aggressively were trying to take market share. When my company negotiated a contract with one of the seven divisions of MCI, our noncompete agreement was not with AT&T or Sprint or another long-distance carrier. Our noncompete agreement stated that we could not sell our services to any of the other MCI divisions. Cutthroat, right? MCI compared performance between its divisions and then rewarded the divisions that performed better. This example is a version of what subtly or not so subtly occurs within companies. Buyers may be afraid that buying your service or product will create issues with another department or division.

THE CHASM OF CHANGE

All of these fears often exist in what I call the Chasm of Change. This chasm is the distance between now and the better future. The Chasm of Change is a deep pit of fears that must be addressed in a language that creates a sense of safety within which senior executive buyers can approve a decision. You don't just need the senior executive buyer to approve, you also need the rest of the buying team to say yes, or at the very least to not say no. In the world of big sales, the power of one of the members of the buying team to say no is more powerful than even the senior executive buyer's ability to say yes. You must assume every person on their team has veto power, and someone vetoes when they think the risks outweigh the benefits. That is, they are afraid of something. Make them feel confident that the Chasm of Change is crossable.

"The power of one of the members of the buying team to say no is more powerful than even the senior executive buyer's ability to say yes"

I remember a time when chief executive officers, owners, and other senior buyers could make decisions on their own. You could talk to them, explain the benefits of what you were selling, answer some questions, provide a proposal, and then they would buy on their own! You would work with your company and team, and they would move everything forward. Your buyer would go to their team and do the same thing. The purchase was rarely questioned because the boss had said to get this new vendor solution on board and make things happen. The change of one vendor or solution over to your company was not a big deal. Okay, it wasn't exactly that easy, but it was a lot less complex than it is now. Technology, compliance, and interdepartmental collaboration all have become more prominent and intricate. All the while, modern leadership declares, "Make mistakes! Try new things! Think outside the box!" as they also stomp on every approach that doesn't work. Overall, this complexity has led to a widened Chasm of Change, filled with skepticism, hesitancy, and plain ol' fear.

The better you get at understanding the perceived complications and identifying who on the buyer's team is feeling the friction, the more smoothly the process will go.

HOW TO IDENTIFY THE FEARFUL

You first must determine who is fearful, how fearful they are, and what they are afraid of. Here are a few ways to know if someone is fearful.

→ **Repeated Questions**

A great sign of engagement is when senior executive buyers or buying teams ask questions. However, when the same question is repeated over several meetings or conversations, it tells you that they are afraid. It is a sore spot with some bad history. Possibly it is an area that you need to cover more thoroughly or in a different way.

→ **Delegation**

When you are delegated downward, it means that the delegator doesn't see the problem you are addressing as big enough of an issue to need to be resolved now. When you are delegated laterally, it means that the person delegating you wants to offset the risk of working with you. Often, salespeople interpret the delegation as an issue of the person's area of responsibility, but it's actually a risk shift.

→ **Resistance**

The frontal attack is at least honest. I have respect for it. However, often the fearful express their concerns when you are not in the room. This resistance then shifts from aggressively curious to unwilling to yield when the resistance happens in every communication regardless of your answer. The fears are deep and most often they are not about you.

→ **Schedule Stretch**

When meetings are delayed, or there is a great deal of rescheduling of your requests for information, it is an indication of fear. It shows the desire of the fearful to avoid a choice or decision by running out the clock.

→ **Ghosting**

When the buyer's team goes quiet suddenly, you have lost their attention. Something safer to do, including doing nothing at all—ghosting—has appeared and pushed you out of consideration.

An advertising company had presented a complete approach to an automotive manufacturer for rolling out the next year's vehicles. It would have earned the advertising company the status of agency of record, a big deal in the advertising world. It was time for final revisions and pricing for the program. Suddenly, a wall goes up. No return of calls or emails at any level, even from prospect personnel who had been informative during the sales process. This went on for three weeks. A certified letter was sent to the advertising company that the contract had been awarded to another company. Who got scared? The manufacturer's marketing department wanted to stay with the current advertising company even though they did not really believe that the competitor was doing a good job. Rather than admit the decision, the manufacturer ghosted the advertising company, and then said in effect, "Don't call us, we'll call you."

"When you are delegated laterally, it means that the person delegating you wants to offset the risk of working with you"

When you experience these behaviors in the sales process, you should keep notes of who, what, where, why, and when. Understanding the fear present in the sales process will give you a high-level view of what your obstacles are to closing the deal.

THE EEL IN THE DEAL

There is an eel in every deal. An eel is someone who is against doing your deal—either now, ever, or at the size that you have proposed. It is important to understand their reasons in order to set your strategy on how to address their threat.

Protecting Status Quo

Lower Influence — Protecting Status Quo

SYMPTOMS
- Ask many small detail questions
- Reference past non-relevant implementation failures
- Advocate smaller bites
- Advocate longer onboarding cycles

SOLUTIONS
- Summarize/group questions to provide answers
- Reference transition map and case studies of transition success
- Set minimum size initial implementation for valuable measurable results
- Reference safety of transition maps

Higher Influence — Protecting Status Quo

SYMPTOMS
- Delay decision date or extend current provider contract
- Reduce priority of changing
- Increase anticipated friction cost of change

SOLUTIONS
- Demonstrate ease of transition map and speed of first realized benefit
- Show gross and net impact of profit if possible
- Provide clear friction cost calculator (value threshold)

Lower Influence ← → Higher Influence

Lower Influence — Protecting Alternative Solution

SYMPTOMS
- Challenge your true understanding of unique business or culture
- Recruit larger numbers of disbelievers
- Focus on similarity to past successful implementations of other initiatives
- Credentialize competitor with your own or your colleagues' past experience

SOLUTIONS
- Demonstrate understanding through use of language and referent endorsements
- Work through 360 degree sessions of assessment to uncover and address issues
- Compose similar successful implementations 1:1
- References

Higher Influence — Protecting Alternative Solution

SYMPTOMS
- Avoid/delay Meetings
- "See more" questions on key benefits of competitor (land mines)
- Disagree with or challenge case studies
- Repeatedly change buying criteria

SOLUTIONS
- Work through agenda, have meetings with decision makers, and send notes
- Identify out of scope questions and separate within scope and answer in addendum
- Break case studies into the 3-5 demonstrated capabilities illustrated
- Establish buying criteria and review at each meeting

Protecting Alternative Solution

EXERCISE Identify which quadrant your eel is in and the actions you're going to take to solve the problem.

THE FEARBREAKERS

THE SIX FEARBREAKERS

The goal of fearbreakers is not to just generally reassure people or indirectly demonstrate that they should feel confident; rather, they need to have their fears specifically addressed and preempted. Once you identify a fear or set of fears, you can deploy fearbreakers—usually a combination of several—to allay the fears and move the deal forward.

1. People

If your team is made up of people with a proven track record and impressive resumes, you're already using people for fearbreaking. Your team needs to be a good match to the buyer's team without being threatening in their expertise. This will ensure that everyone is speaking the same language and making meaningful business connections.

I worked on a multibillion-dollar agreement between a drug patent holder and an organization vying to manufacture and distribute the drug. The buying team had key people on it—chemists, drug compliance specialists, operations personnel, lawyers, and the CFO. The selling team arranged for a full two days of meetings. Through those two days, the selling company rotated various members of its own team during meetings and conversations with the buying team. They had dinner together, had some wine, had some laughs, told some stories, and by the end of the second day, the sale was made. The key was not having a sales professional be the face of the company but the experts who would be doing the work. In this way, presenting the right people could be enough to break the buyer's fear.

2. Process

Process reassures companies that you have the necessary approach, documentation, and methodology that can be followed to repeatedly meet the buying company's needs. If you are selling paint to an equipment manufacturer for their machinery, they want to know the process you use for color-verifying that the pigment is right. They'll want to know your quality control processes, supply-chain management, disaster recovery plans, and every other impacting process. And that's just for paint! Why do they need it? Because your ability to demonstrate process and the experience it represents means that you are speaking the language of a big sale. They can then have more confidence in you.

In one instance, an Italian meat manufacturer was selling to a very large national distribution company. The buying company wanted to talk about supply chain, volume, quality assured by the FDA, and so on. A book-size file of documents and information was sent to the buying company, but they still had questions. In turn, the buyers were invited out to the facility in person and walked through every step of the process and also met the FDA inspector on site. The tour started at the loading dock where the ingredients came in and then followed a piece of pork from that door all the way to being loaded onto a truck going out to market. Instead of answering their questions endlessly, they broke the buyer's fear by literally showing them how the sausage was made.

3. Technology

You can break fears with novel introductions of technology into products. Up-to-date technology makes people confident that a product is transparent, monitorable, analyzable, and reliable.

A pressure gauge manufacturer I worked with was selling their "at distance" pressure technology. This rather basic Bluetooth technology allowed refining operation managers to know that all gauges in the refinery provided by the manufacturer were within proper standards. This simple addition, and the salesperson's bringing attention to it, created the sense that the technology would provide a sense of transparency, control, and safety.

Technology is a great fearbreaker for small companies selling to bigger companies that might be worried about the selling team's sophistication or scalability. Seeking out impressive software and novel technologies will go a long way toward offering big value for your big sale.

4. Experience

Few people want to be the first company to buy something new. Especially someone buying a big sale from a company smaller than they are. That is why experience is so important as a fearbreaker. Telling the stories of what has happened in the past and what you learned from that gives a clear picture of the experience that you and your team have.

A food machinery distributor was looking to introduce new equipment into the market. The production company that got the deal did so by sharing tons of stories about the different generations of equipment they had seen and created over the years. The seller was able to show their expertise and passion via their vast experience making and improving the equipment.

5. Collaboration

Buyers who buy big sales want to be involved all the way to the end of the process. By inviting and including members of the buying team through the pre-proposal phase of the sales process, you allow them to take responsibility for some of the solution without having to take sole accountability. Even if the collaboration is not really necessary for the submission of a proposal, creating a way for there to be a collaborative event will still have a big impact on the acceptance of a final proposal because all of the stakeholders will have a proud sense of ownership and involvement in the process.

A medical device company was taking a new joint replacement product into the marketplace. They held collaborative design and training development sessions with the largest groups of joint replacement practices. Presentations were made to the collected surgeons, then breakout groups discussed how to make the joint replacement product better for both the surgeon using the product and for the recovery of the patient. When it came to market, many of the doctors who would be using the product had already provided input into the device. It had, in part, become their designed device.

"**Creating a way for there to be a collaborative event will have a big impact on the acceptance of a final proposal because all of the stakeholders will have a proud sense of ownership and involvement in the process**"

6. Control

How does a buyer make certain that if a purchase is not producing the desired result, they can slow down or stop the work until the problem is fixed? Contracts can create a sense of "after the fact" comfort, but that is not the kind of fear-removal that buyers want. If anything, these contractual additions add to people's fears that things will go wrong. Instead, they want to know what adjustments can be made in real time to keep things moving. These controls can come through either meetings, regular updates, or reporting, all of which make the buyers feel like they are still at the helm.

For instance, a buyer was looking for a company in China to make a large number of parts, but they were concerned about quality, adherence to procedure, and use of the equipment. They were very nervous because the manufacturing plant was halfway around the world. The company in China proposed having cameras on all of the machines and gauges, and work process with live feeds and time stamps. The normal reports, QC procedures, and other standard operation protections would also be in place. The buyer's team loved it. They would be "right on the shop floor" when the parts were being made. They signed the contract. Importantly, the US company stopped checking the feed after three weeks. They didn't need to have constant observation, they just needed to feel that they had the control to have it as an option.

Sales of any kind are ruined by fearful buyers. Learn to identify and neutralize fears while ensuring that you close your deals at a higher rate, and that they close with less drama. Instead of being afraid of the fears and worrying that they will ruin your deals, take them as opportunities to walk through the Authority Arc (see Chapter 2) again and again until your expertise and deep insight address your buyer's fears from all angles.

⭐ Key Takeaways

1. The identifiable categories of fear that affect buying decisions on the part of the executive buyer are accountability, change, friction, work, and mistakes (see page 60).

2. Fear must be neutralized, reduced, or eliminated for the sales message and benefits to truly be heard and agreed upon (see page 60).

3. Fears are more important than benefits. Benefits create interest, fears make decisions (see page 62).

4. There are six fearbreakers for overcoming a buyer's fears: people, process, technology, experience, collaboration, and control. Using one or several in combination is effective at reducing the buyer's fear so that the buyer can listen and understand your sales value (see page 68).

5. Find more relevant resources at TheSecretToBigSales.com.

CHAPTER

4

Your Senior Executive Buyer

Identify and secure your senior executive buyer for a speedy and smooth sales process.

Your senior executive buyer is your main point of contact and the key person you need to get on board with your offering. By way of a framework, we'll start with a script showing how your first meeting with a senior executive buyer could go. Based off this script, I'll walk you through the language, promises, and confirmations you must explicitly seek out before spending time and resources pursuing the sale.

FIRST CONTACT

In big sales, a single meeting will not yield a big sale. However, your first contact is integral to the rest of the process. The goals of your first contact should be:

1. Determine if there is a challenge that you can solve and how fast the prospect needs it solved.
2. Establish the actions that the prospect is willing to execute for this sales process.
3. Confirm a second meeting that includes the buying team.

In the first meeting, you are expected to already know your executive sponsor's concerns. By stating the types of problems that your company solves and asking if the buyer has one or more of those, you have positioned yourself to the buyer as a relevant person prepared to discuss the true issues that the buyer and their company are facing. Preparation for the meeting includes understanding the prospect's industry and their executive-level challenges. This is how you can speak past your product and solution.

In the dialogue below, I lay out how a first meeting may go down. You'll notice how little time and effort is spent on selling your company's capabilities and solutions. The conversation should be aimed at the prospect's issues and relevant responses about your company's understanding of the issues and willingness to have a meeting to discuss the "hows" of implementation. Senior executive buyers for big sales are only partially interested in "how." Their expectation is that their team will examine the *how*—they care about *what* they will receive from working with your company.

Senior Sales Professional: Thanks for the meeting time. I sent an agenda ahead of time. Have you had a chance to review it?

Senior Executive Buyer: I glanced at it.

Senior Sales Professional: The key outcome that I am hoping we can decide is if there is a reason to have another meeting. If we are a good fit for the challenges you have, we should. If not, we should invest our time elsewhere. Did you have any other outcomes you wanted for today's meeting?

Senior Executive Buyer: I'd like to learn more about your company.

Senior Sales Professional: Of course. Our company helps companies like yours—those between $200 million and $500 million in size in the manufacturing industry—to solve one or more of the following three problems:

→ Take their products to market thirty to ninety days faster than their current rate
→ Reduce waste by 3%–11%
→ Create flexibility in the design process so that market applications can increase for identified new markets

Do you have any of those challenges?

Senior Executive Buyer: Well, kind of. Our overall margins are affected mostly by quality issues at the end of manufacturing. We do re-work on our products over 4% of the time. It kills our margins. If you call that waste, then that's what we have. Although, because we re-work the product after production we don't refer to it as waste. Materials deemed unusable through manufacturing we call waste. We have good flexibility, it's one of the things we are known for. We are beating market averages for speed to customer after sale. The thing I'm concerned about is that if we get a big order, it is more likely that we will have a higher re-work rate. It's our margin killer.

> **"Senior executive buyers for big sales are only partially interested in 'how.' Their expectation is that their team will examine the *how*—they care about *what* they will receive from working with your company"**

Senior Sales Professional: Yeah, in your industry, demand fluctuations and design changes are driving the re-work percentages up because there is little time to develop full in-process protocols. You're a little bit better than most at 4% though.

Senior Executive Buyer: That's a big part of it. It's also an issue of getting the labor trained up on each adjustment to the end-product shifts. We have everything set up accurately and another opportunity comes in. We're very profitable and part of it is because we can accept whatever comes in, within reason. I just want to knock out the re-work and pick up a few more profit points.

Senior Sales Professional: We can help fix that—we have a technology for in-process quality measures and we move them to a dashboard for adjustments.

Senior Executive Buyer: We already have our own production line processes for measuring quality and to make adjustments.

Senior Sales Professional: That's good, most top manufacturers do. That's why you have a 96% positive manufacture pass-through number. The last 4% is what we help fix. We work with a proprietary machine learning system to rapidly tweak and help manage the points of unacceptable performance to move any of your lines closer to the 100% pass-through. It's a rapid-learning system using many of the gauges you already have. We add a few of our own measuring devices, put this through our technology, and help you and your team make real-time adjustments. For some companies that make the same things without much adjustment, over and over again, we don't offer as much benefit. For a company like yours that wants to accept any job that comes, making changes is part of your competitive advantage and that makes us a great fit.

Senior Executive Buyer: I'm definitely interested. Send me a proposal and I'll look at it.

Senior Sales Professional: We don't really know what we're proposing on yet. Here is our process to make certain that we have a thorough and accurate proposal. First, we secure an executive sponsor, in this case that would probably be you. We meet with your team and our team on a peer-to-peer basis to examine all of the particulars of the potential proposal. We all meet and review findings and agree upon tweaks to the overall approach. Then we submit a proposal.

Senior Executive Buyer: It sounds like a lot of work just to get a proposal.

Senior Sales Professional: Maybe—but you know that the first 96% is very hard, but the last 4% we help you fix is all profit margin. If it flows straight to the bottom line, it's worth getting fixed.

Senior Executive Buyer: It sounds like you need to talk to some of our people.

Senior Sales Professional: And it sounds like you are our executive sponsor. The role means that you have the problem that needs to be solved and you would like it fixed quickly. Besides that, it means that you are one of the signatures on the final contract.

Senior Executive Buyer: This is my company; I am the only signature.

Senior Sales Professional: Great. I need to keep you in the loop as we meet with your people to keep you up to date about the progress. I ask that you give me a list of the people who need to be involved and their contact information so we can reach out. The first meeting for the process I'd like you to set so that everyone knows the initiative is important. There may be some logjams along the ways, at which point I'll reach out for your help. We should be able to move from now to proposal within three to six weeks if we get your support this way.

Senior Executive Buyer: That all sounds reasonable. But I need some case studies from you before I agree to this.

Senior Sales Professional: I understand. I brought five with me for the meeting just in case they would be helpful.

Senior Executive Buyer: Okay—let's set a tentative date for the first meeting with the team for next week on Thursday or Friday. I'll have my support person work through the calendars to see when.

Senior Sales Professional: I'll bring my peer-to-peer team members to the meeting as well. I'm looking forward to this. I think we can be a great help to your company.

That is fundamentally how a big sales conversation works. That's the language, the positioning, the ask, and the meeting control. Of course, there are lots of nuances and adjustments you will make with your own industry and prospects, but structurally, this is the language and flow that you should use in a first meeting.

⏱ Be the Crystal Ball

Many senior executive buyers are paid to predict the future. You are selling an outcome, not a process. Importantly, this shouldn't be done with general statements such as "I'm concerned with what is coming down the line" or "Inflation is going to make your costs rise." These don't help your senior executive buyer make the right choice. In providing specific predictions, you can bring credibility to yourself and your company. Each prediction should include exact numbers as well as your recommendation. Some examples include:

→ "The double-digit inflation in your raw materials will continue. However, there is a softening in the component expense area. You will be able to take advantage of that in your pricing."

→ "Hacking efforts have increased fivefold in the past year. The challenge that companies like yours face is that protection efforts have barely changed. Your enemies are working five times as hard to take your data than you are to defend it."

→ "Housing starts are estimated to drop by 6% per month for each of the next six months. We're advising you to step away from your focus on residential materials to commercial materials and secure the contracts rather than waiting the six months."

THE MUST-HAVES

The three must-haves are discovered and confirmed in the first meeting. If any of the must-haves are not present, you can be sure it's not the right time or buyer for you.

1. A Big Problem

You can always identify big problems with these three characteristics:

A. They are the type of problem that, if solved, will move the performance needle of the buyer or company by 5% or more.

B. The scale of the problem has visibility beyond the executive buyer. In other words, others know that it is a problem, and it needs to be solved.

C. The solutions to big problems cannot be purchased by just one person. The problem must be big enough that it requires other people within that company to participate in the consideration of a presented solution. No one buys alone.

2. Authority

You need to make sure your prospect is the person responsible for signing off on what you are selling. Sometimes you'll ask and be told, "Just me! I'm the one in charge." Then, down the line, you'll hear something frustrating like, "Hold on, I've got to take this up the chain first." Authority is critical not just because you want to be interfacing with the person who signs, but you also want the person who can take the necessary steps to bring the deal to a close—including the five behaviors on page 84. If you want to learn who has the actual authority as efficiently and clearly as possible, you must ask specific questions about the process. Learn more about this in Chapter 7.

I learned the issue of true authority the hard way. My selling team and I had developed a solution for a credit card processing company that would save them millions of dollars and accelerate their services to their customers. It was beautiful. We thought our executive sponsor had the authority to sign the contract. She said she did. We verified this at every step in our sales process. At the final step for signature, she tells us that she has to take this to the CFO. We had no opportunity up until that point to present our solution or demonstrate its impact. The CFO, blind to us and with no understanding of what we were proposing, refused the contract and would not see us for presentation. The VP, who was our executive sponsor, had the interest but not the authority.

3. Urgency

Your buyer needs to have a deadline, ideally under sixty days. It depends on the industry—for instance, construction or engineering services usually take ninety days—but it's vital that your buyer needs your service fast, whatever fast means to them. Urgency is a measure of engagement and communicates to you that it is a top-three priority for them to implement. You must encourage your buyer to state this urgency explicitly, and if they cannot, you should come back at a later date when it has moved up in priority.

Notice that all three of these must-haves require you to ask questions. This is not about you selling yet, this is you qualifying. You should procure these must-haves in order as well, as each one will inform the next.

❓ What Is an Executive, Anyway?

An executive, at a high level, has the following responsibilities regardless of their purview:

1. They decide where to spend capital, which includes hiring, expanding facilities, partnerships, and how to commit resources to grow the business.

2. They decide the culture, which includes a declaration of principles as well as what actions are worth rewarding or not.

3. They decide the team, which includes hiring and firing to grow the business.

4. They decide what choices to make, which includes any decisions or route that creates or modifies the business's strategy.

Will what you are selling meet the threshold for items 1 and 4 on this list? It must, otherwise your solution likely doesn't solve a high-priority problem for them and they will defer, deny, delegate, or delay.

"Your buyer needs to have a deadline, ideally under sixty days"

CONFIRMING ACTIONS

Now that your buyer is qualified, you can begin the selling process. The measure of real engagement of a senior executive buyer is their willingness to agree to five actions and then execute them. Without these five actions, your solution is possibly interesting but still unsupported. In the script at the beginning of this chapter, all five of these commitments were asked for and agreed to. They weren't "kinda" asked for. They were asked for specifically. When it comes to communicating with senior executive buyers, you cannot infer their commitment. The senior executive buyer's job, after all, is to commit resources and make choices. You need to make certain that their interest is strong enough to agree to each of these:

1. **Provide Access**

    To establish the possibility of selling in a peer-to-peer environment, you need to have access to the buying team. You need an organization chart, identified members, and their contact information. It is reassuring to the senior executive buyer that you are handling this for them. Even though they'll be sending out the introductory email on your behalf, it's important you understand who everyone is and how to contact them as the deal progresses. Furthermore, access also includes information—files, policies, presentations, and documents that are vital and relevant to the success of the project.

2. **Set Priority**

    In the introductory email, and throughout the deal's communications, your senior executive buyer must let the buying team know that you will be getting in touch, and that it is a priority to participate in the evaluation and discussion process. This makes access more likely and easier.

3. **Give Clarity**

    When working with a larger company on a bigger challenge, things may happen that you don't quite understand. Perhaps key information is being kept off-limits. Perhaps there is an initiative that precedes yours. Maybe personnel shifts are anticipated and not widely known. When something regarding the peer-to-peer process becomes confusing, the senior executive buyer must provide clarity so that you can figure out how to move forward. If the senior executive buyer has stated that they will help when clarity is necessary, you can figure out how to move forward.

"The senior executive buyer's job, after all, is to commit resources and make choices"

4. Stay in the Loop

Set a weekly or bimonthly fifteen-minute check-in with the senior executive buyer to discuss progress. Without an open channel of communication, it is possible for you to drift off the priority list and languish in the slipping calendar of your sales process.

5. Break Logjams

In a big sale, there can be passive or active resistance from people on the buyer's team. You will know it is happening because meetings are being rescheduled, key members are showing up late or leaving early, and it is suddenly difficult to get important information or documents. These are logjams. Along the way, you will need to point these out to the senior executive buyer as a part of your regular call. This isn't because it's their job, it's because they are the one person with the authority to break the logjams. Your senior executive buyer told you that it was a big challenge, that they had the authority to make it happen, and that the resolution was urgent. The senior executive buyer should be as anxious to break that logjam as you are. If you can't get them to do this, you will have a much lower close ratio.

🔑 Working Backward from the CFO

If you can relieve the CFO's fears, or even get them excited, everything else will be much easier. For some reason, it took me a long time to realize that every big sale would cross a CFO's desk before approval. But of course, if my company was going to solve a big problem, then our proposal would have a financial measure in one way or another. I went through many pertinent money terms in Chapter 1, but how and when do you leverage them?

1. As soon as you identify your senior executive buyer, ask to have a meeting with the CFO.
2. Meet with the CFO and discuss the measures that you are working with for the evaluation of the work process and to find out what exactly they are working on to improve their financial performance.
3. Using the language from Chapter 1, discuss the pertinent areas that your solution would impact. These areas could be revenue, market growth cost, margin, net margin, or any other business vitals.
4. Ask for the opportunity to meet again along the way to discuss progress.

I remember being in a meeting with five or six other senior executives from a prospect company to make our proposal presentation. This was the first time we had met the CFO. He was not a particularly pleasant person—no smile, little eye contact, and mostly grunts as the presentation started. We were not even ten minutes in when he stopped the meeting and said, "I don't need to hear about all of what you are presenting." He gestured to his team, "These guys will figure out if it is worthwhile. What I need to know is how much it will cost, how much we will receive in revenue or savings, and how soon. If you can't tell me that, you won't see me again."

"You'll find those exact numbers on slide 11 in the deck you have," I responded. He looked at it. Then he looked up and said, "These numbers work. Now you figure out if these numbers are real or if they are just smoke." Then he left with the deck. We finished the rest of our presentation, but the conversation transformed from a pitch presentation into a collaboration with the team to make sure the numbers worked for the CFO.

BE SPECIFIC

I have spent a lot of time with companies that offer soft benefits instead of hard numbers. For example, a company that sells organizational culture development might say: "If you hire us, then people will be on the same page and happier and they will produce more and stay longer." For the selling company this is probably true, and they know they have been impactful in the past. The issue is, CFOs don't like soft, correlational benefits, even if the CEO is excited. Below you'll find some examples of how, during your first meetings, you can *translate* soft benefits into hard numbers. Those numbers should be precise and relevant.

Scenario 1: Construction Company

Soft: "Companies hire us because we deliver your project on time and on budget."

Hard: "Companies hire us because they have an active work site for greater than sixteen hours per day. Those companies need the project exactly on time and on budget. Historically, we deliver ahead of schedule on an average of fifteen to forty-five days. That's the period of time from signature to occupancy."

The revised statement includes important terminology and hard numbers, which connote that the selling company understands the problem at a deep level. "Active work site," "greater than sixteen hours per day," "ahead of schedule on an average of fifteen to forty-five days" all demonstrate a grasp of the specifics. Even the last sentence, "That's the period of time from signature to occupancy," implies a number. It shows a level of confidence, relevance, and expertise that a senior executive buyer does not hear very often when talking to a possible contractor. The numbers do not feel like general claims.

Scenario 2: Manufacturer

Soft: "Companies buy from us because our products meet all of the specifications of your original drawings, and our quality performance is at 99.999%."

Hard: "Companies buy from us when they need the speed and flexibility to take defined requirement to manufactured part in less than ten working days; scalability and flexibility of order volumes varying as much as twofold on a month-to-month basis without surcharges; and market-standard quality performance of 99.999%."

The hard numbers here achieve many ends, including throwing competitors under the bus by noting with a wink that the 99.999% quality is just the market standard and therefore doesn't need to be considered that much of a selling point. Instead, the hard numbers here precisely state that the price will stay in check and the products will be delivered on time.

Scenario 3: Professional Supply Chain Management

Soft: "We provide an end-to-end evaluation of your supply chain, and we find those opportunities to increase efficiency and eliminate bottlenecks."

Hard: "The term supply chain is really inaccurate. A chain implies that all the pieces are of the same weight and importance. It's not true. An example is that there is a general understanding that China is shipping product at 60% less than pre-pandemic levels. We ask these questions as a part of our evaluation and velocity of your 'speed to serving' challenge:

→ During times of inventory reduction, such as China's ability to meet only 60% of the demand in the marketplace, there are winners and losers on the purchasing side. Not all of the buyers of Chinese-produced products or materials will be reduced to 60%. Some buyers will receive closer to 100%, while other buyers will receive less than 60%. We develop the suppliers, contracts, and controls to put our customers in the best position during supply chain interruption.

"CFOs don't like soft, correlational benefits, even if the CEO is excited"

→ Our clients set their production schedules based upon less than thirty-six-hour increments. The materials must be available with 100% confidence within at least thirty-six hours of need. If not, there will need to be a changeover of the production line to another product or their production line will have to shut down. When a company does not have at least thirty-six-hour absolute confidence, you cannot manage the velocity at which you run your production line. That means slowing it down. Our clients use our proprietary visibility software to track, flag, and provide work-around solutions to keep production moving.

→ The other side of the challenge is too much inventory. Your policies of 'just in time' make certain that your facilities are efficient because excess materials are not filling every space. Our approach controls both sides of the deficiency and excess of supply management."

The discussion moved from general claims that any other provider should be able to offer, to what the senior executive buyer would receive as benefit and how it would impact their operation. Notice that there isn't a reference to the specific product or existing system. The statements are the highest level of consideration. The numbers are important and highly relevant.

When selling big, you've got to always be answering your senior executive buyer's biggest question: "Do you, vendor, actually understand my challenge?"

If you want to win the deal, your response must include numbers, precision, and relevance.

At every turn you must translate your "sale speak" into language that your buyer will understand, and more importantly that will make them feel understood. They don't need your 99.999% promises, they want the nitty-gritty numbers and the confidence that tells them exactly how working with you is going to move the dial on things they care about.

⭐ Key Takeaways

1. Senior executive buyers value your ability to "tell the future." As an expert, part of your role is to project potential paths that the future of their business or industry will follow (see page 80).

2. Senior executive buyers are qualified by having a big problem, authority to make the buying decision, and the urgency to get the problem solved (see page 80).

3. The actions necessary for a senior executive buyer to perform are as follows: provide access, set priority, give clarity, stay in the loop, and break logjams. If they cannot or will not do these, they are not committed to the effort of evaluating your value (see page 84).

4. Be specific and numeric in the value of your offering when working with senior executive buyers (see page 87).

5. Find more relevant resources at TheSecretToBigSales.com.

CHAPTER

5

The Leadership Layer Cake

Understand how every role in an organization has a different worldview, and how that should inform the language you use.

To land big sales, you'll have to talk to all sorts of people at many levels of an organization. Talking to each is like cutting through a layer cake, with each layer having new characteristics and textures. If you don't change your language for every level of concern, you will not have maximum impact. While it is natural to believe that the best overall solution for a prospect wins, it's not true. Let's dive into *how* exactly to change your language depending on your prospect's position.

Organizational charts all differ company to company. They differ by title, authority, and function. We once received an email from a person with the title of director of customer happiness. It's warm, fuzzy, clever, cute, but not particularly helpful if I am deciding whether they are the right person to sell to. You'll come across a lot of titles that are a bit unclear like this. We were once selling to a company with $500 million in annual revenue. It had seven different presidents! And that wasn't because there were different divisions, markets, or product lines. Along the way, someone came up with the idea that the title president of something was empowering—president of customer delight, president of partner involvement, president of making it right. I wish I was kidding, but I'm not. What do you sell to the president of partner involvement? We could guess, but we don't really know from the outside.

We use a tool called the Layer Cake to orient ourselves in new organizational environments. This way, we're able to understand what motivates each person, and therefore what words to use when selling to them.

Even though titles may differ from company to company, we are going to be using the four traditional leadership titles that most people fall under: president, vice president, director, and manager. As shown in the Layer Cake below, for each of these titles, there are five motivation categories you need to identify to understand how to best speak to them in words they understand: (1) ambition, (2) time scale, (3) value concerns, (4) buying concerns, and (5) tenure.

By looking at each of the four titles through the lens of these five motivation categories, you can learn what the language of the big sale is for each of these key players. Let's dive in.

	Position	Ambition	Time Scale	Value Concerns	Buying Concerns	Tenure
NON-BUDGET FUNDED	President/ CEO	Build resume in key area of reputation	Annually, 18 month, and 24 month	Move needles Public or board problems	Select from options	<3 Years
SOFT-BUDGET FUNDED	VPs	Survive regime change	Quarterly and Annually	Unique Knowledge Risk control	Consensus Assign Slow-walk	5+ Years
SOFT-BUDGET FUNDED	Directors	Move up to VP or out to VP	Monthly and Quarterly	Fast, Flashy Low risk, done before	Proven elsewhere Ease/ Speed to implement	3-5 Years
BUDGET FUNDED	Managers	Move to Director	<Monthly	Relationship Cheaper	Process Budget	5+ Years

THE FOUR POSITIONS

1. President

There are two types of presidents: hired from the inside and hired from the outside. At a $500 million company, about half the time presidents are promoted from within, and the other half they are hired from outside.

It's important that you know where your president (or CEO) was hired from because they have different viewpoints depending on where they came from. If they were hired from the inside, they were brought on to keep things moving as they were. If they were hired from the outside, it's because there is a problem that needs fixing.

From the outside: If the board of directors wants to make a change, they know it most likely can't come from the inside. For instance, this might happen when the board wants to expand into new markets or product lines or if they want to find someone who can divest assets at the maximum value. People are also hired from outside if there are simply no good options available within the company and they want some fresh energy.

From the inside: There are always people working at a company for years or decades hoping that they will be rewarded with the brass ring. This sort of person is usually promoted to president or CEO if the desire is to just keep the boat running and on course. This promotion can look many different ways. Maybe the right person has been groomed for six to twelve months to take on the role in stride. Maybe it's a generational hire where legacy drives the decision. Other times, there is a belief, accurate or not, that the value of the culture precedes all other criteria and so someone is promoted because of cultural alignment.

Regardless, it's important to try to glean this information up front (if you can't find it online). Very often, in a first meeting with a president or CEO we ask the question in this way.

"CEOs or presidents like you are brought in to solve a problem or initiate a significant change in the business. What problem or issue brought you here?"

Direct? Gutsy? Maybe, however, I have found that the senior executive buyers who are open to buying big will answer this question with specificity. The language of big sales is not about the words alone, it's about when and how to use them.

2. Vice President

VPs can be challenging. They can be a springboard or an elephant's graveyard. They are often trying to just hit their numbers and cover their backs. I once spoke to a group of VPs and senior VPs of Fortune 100 companies and said that VPs are always in a civil yet hostile war over resources and credit. One of the attendees, who couldn't stop laughing, came up to us after the meeting and said, "I just retired from [top Fortune 20 company], and a I spent a third of my time pushing our shortfall over onto other departments, taking credit for successes, and pushing revenues and expenses into different months so that my numbers hit budget."

I said, "Did you ever get penalized for it?"
"No, everyone knew the game."
"Were you trying to become president?"
"God no!" he exclaimed. "President means you will last twenty to thirty months."

VPs are looking to do well, keep their jobs, and bet on the sure thing. They are not looking to make risky decisions. This means that they are often very cautious in what changes they'll sign on to. They need to collect credit if the purchase from you works. They also need to have a target to deflect onto or share responsibility with if it does not. I have on occasion, and not so gently, referred to vice presidents in big companies as the "cockroaches of leadership." Their big and greatest desire is survival. Their second desire is advancement. Their third desire is to get hired away to another company for more money and authority as a vice president.

3. Director

All hat, no cattle. They have the ambition for improvement and change. Their first desire is to be recognized as uniquely capable of making a difference. Their second desire is advancement. Their third desire is to get hired away to another company for more money and authority as a vice president. They are difficult in the sales process because they declare that they have authority to make a buying decision when they do not. Often, you are then warned not to go around them to anyone else.

"**VPs are looking to do well, keep their jobs, and bet on the sure thing. They are not looking to make risky decisions**"

4. Manager

Big sales are not sold at the manager level. Period. Often, managers are vendor swapping rather than looking for unique value. Even if a manager increases the amount of whatever they are buying, this is not "selling," this is just an increase in volume or taking a share of another vendor's portion.

👀 Read the Room!

Warren Buffett once said, "If you sit down to a hand of poker and in three deals you don't know who the chump is, get up, you're the chump." Every meeting with the buyer's team is the same. When you sit down for a meeting with the buyer's team, you need to identify four characters in the room:

→ **Senior Executive Buyer:** The senior executive buyer who invited you to the room and has met all of the criteria we have already discussed in Chapter 4.

→ **Eel in the Deal:** Every deal has an eel. An eel is anyone from the buyer's team who wants to get in the way of your closing your sale with the buyer's team now, as discussed in Chapter 3.

→ **Friendly Buyer:** This person is responsive and shows positive indications that they like what you are presenting.

→ **The Spy:** You are always looking for a spy. A spy gives you information that you would not otherwise get and that is information they will not give to other competitors.

THE FIVE MOTIVATION CATEGORIES

Every one of these positions is motivated by different factors. The purpose of understanding their categories of motivation is to deliver a narrative of interest that speaks to the person's integrated set of concerns.

1. Ambition

The misconception is that all positions within a company want to do well and help the company to grow. Ha! That is usually *somewhere* on the list of motivations. However, it is often not first. My brother used to say, "I trust everyone to do what they believe to be in their own best interest." It's not necessarily a bad thing, but it is key to using the right words to appeal to people's specific desires. Across organizations, you can be sure that ambitions are very different between the management levels.

→ **Manager:** Their ambition is to move up.
  They want enough money to pay their bills plus one more thing. That one thing could be education for their children, taking care of a sick relative, a new car, a cabin—anything. Their ambition is to move up and afford life, and then some.

→ **Director:** Up or out.
  Directors see themselves like associates at a law firm. An associate lawyer either makes partner within five to seven years, or they move to another firm with the desire to make partner there. For directors, it is always a stepping stone position. If they can't move to VP within three to five years, they will move on.

→ **Vice President:** Survival of the fittest.
  Every company will reorganize, change leadership, buy, be bought, merge, expand, or contract within eighteen-month cycles. If you are a smart VP in a large company, your job is to hit your numbers, make a difference, and survive regime changes. You may be surprised how many people in these positions *do not* want to advance.

→ **President:** Solve the problem, pull the golden parachute.
  Presidents hired from outside of the company they lead are often problem-assassins. They are in the position to fix a significant organizational issue. There is a reason that presidents of publicly held organizations are more interested in negotiating their exit package than they are their hiring package—it's because everybody knows they are leaving.

"Deliver a narrative of interest that speaks to the person's integrated set of concerns"

2. Time Scale

Performance metrics are set differently for the various positions in an organization. The simple rule of thumb is that the higher up the organizational chart you go, the longer the time scale is.

- **Manager:** Monthly
- **Director:** Monthly and quarterly
- **Vice President:** Quarterly and annually
- **President:** Annually.

3. Value Concerns

If you put all four positions in a room at the same time and gave the same presentation, it is possible you would only get one to two favorable responses. That is because there are few truly shared motivations within the variety of positions in a company when making a decision. For the language of big sales, looking at what is valued concerns only the VP and the president. At the level of what is valued, the director and manager will take their direction from the VP's and president's choices.

- **Manager:** They look to the VP and president.

- **Director:** They look to the VP and president.

- **Vice President:** Because the ambition for a VP is survival, they are looking for solutions that leave them in a position of unique value. They are considered the expert in an area and difficult to replace. I have been in discussions with companies that are reorganizing. VPs who "own all the relationships" on either the client, distributor, or customer side are saved in a reorganization. So are the VPs who control a division, whether that is regional, international, or irreplaceable product line. It can be technological understanding, a critical point of failure for supply chain management. Regardless, being unique keeps them safe in a reorg, even if they are less than the best-performing VP in their company. When they buy, they want to see themselves as protected from memorable failure.

→ **President:** They are paid to move the needle, so big sales are great for them if they are big and move big needles. A CEO of a multinational multibillion-dollar company was invited to a meeting for a presentation about a new technology to help with the efficiency of a part of one of the company's operations. When he asked how much it would cost and how much it would yield, the selling company proudly said, "It only costs $10 million and it will yield $100 million over a three-year period." The CEO stood up and stormed out of the room, looking at his executive team and saying, "What the hell am I doing in a $100 million meeting!" Not enough needle would have moved and not fast enough.

4. Buying Concerns

→ **Manager:** They are looking for a great and clear process that hits their target budget.

→ **Director:** They are looking for ease of use, speed of implementation, and a proven track record elsewhere.

→ **Vice President:** They want to stay in the company. They want to claim credit and delegate failure. They want to survive regime change. To do this, they look for consensus because more people who agree also means more people to blame later. They'll want to assign a project leader to be their fall guy. They will slow-walk the project so that they are certain what leadership they are trying to please.

→ **President:** They are busy and do not want to have to dig through all the data, RFP response information, or solution testing. They expect all that work to have been done by their own team before the proposal crosses their desk. Presidents want to set direction and allocate resources. To do this, they want to choose between options on how to solve a problem. They will dive deep into the options and if unsatisfied with the answers, send those options back for more data or clarity. In the end, however, their desire is to have a choice to make from a series of options.

Tenure

VPs want to stay; presidents are preparing to leave. When selling large sales, you are speaking the language of rapid impact and sustained success so that the VP feels safe and the president knows the impact will be attached to their tenure.

- **Manager:** 5 years or more
- **Director:** 3–5 years
- **Vice President:** 5 years or more
- **President:** Less than 3 years

🔵 Stay Out of Politics

Oftentimes, paying attention to every person's particular concerns might lead you dangerously close to getting involved with the internal politics of a company. Whatever you do, do not take sides. Stay out of the politics no matter who in the Layer Cake you're working with.

This means you should never take sides. It is tempting when you are building relationships with a new prospect or customer to listen to the issues that they are having. It's a good thing to do. It builds relationships and provides information. But do not ever help one member of a company in an issue with another member of the company. I've always been surprised at how much solicitation for support occurs from companies of their vendors to back them on a political play inside of their own companies. Stay away; if there is a fight going down, you don't want to pick the wrong fighter.

THREE PITCHES, ONE SALE

Much as in the beginning of Chapter 4, below you'll find dialogue from real conversations with a company selling an integrated inventory management system. There are three conversations with three different high-level employees so you can see the differences in communication style and word usage depending on where each one is in the Layer Cake.

1. DIRECTOR LEVEL

Goal: Ensuring the safety of implementation while not interrupting current workflow.

You: Our system generates a real-time dashboard providing complete visibility to the speed you are going through inventory, if there is an area or a component that has a hire waste rate, and you can customize the reports to meet your needs.

Director: This looks like a lot of work to put together with our internal systems.

You: We work with a lot of companies like yours. That's why we built our system with an open interface. It takes less than six weeks from initial analysis, programming, out-of-system testing, and on-system testing.

Director: What is "out-of-system" testing?

You: With all the companies that we work with, we provide an offline testing period using live-data feeds. This means that none of the active functions are used, but the reporting and scenarios will be visible to you before we start.

Director: Well, if we can test it all out before it goes live, it sounds like something we want to try.

2. VICE PRESIDENT LEVEL

Goal: Ensure they will have control through the process of purchase, implementation, and ongoing work.

You: In your industry, there is a significant amount of waste that occurs because of excessive purchases of materials and components that you then must store and account for. Often, your production line will have changed over to a new product and the leftover components and materials will have to be written off and categorized as waste. Our system gives you visibility and control over materials and component inventory to meet whatever just-in-time threshold you set.

Vice President: Who has access to this information? How are the inputs and outputs managed?

You: The access points and permissions are controlled by whoever you assign as the administrative manager. You can include yourself or others. You can also provide layers of authority. This also includes price points for materials from vendors, vendor approval, and purchase levels. You can even do ratio splits on orders between vendors so that you are not single-sourced.

Vice President: Who else have you done this for that is relevant to our type of company?

You: I have several relevant case studies we can review.

Vice President: Great, send them over. This looks very interesting. Let's get my team to go through how this might work and see if they agree on how we might consider a proposal.

3. PRESIDENT LEVEL

Goal: Ensure they will receive the promised results and that those results are better than what your competitors promise.

You: One of the challenges for manufacturers is the handling of their material and component inventory. Counting it is one thing—most companies such as yours have developed processes for that. The real issue is the excess 1%–4% that is showing up in their work in progress on their balance sheet. This happens when there are components or materials that are no longer needed because the remaining inventory cannot be used for current orders. Often there are over-orders of materials that sit on the shelves or in storage because of a fear of stopping the production line. Just-in-time inventory is a great concept and we are certain that for serving current production lines, many steps have been taken. However, the industry itself and our work with clients still shows 1%–4% over-ordered or unnecessary materials and components held inside of your balance sheet. This is a month-over-month waste.

President: What will it take to do a diagnostic of our inventory? I want to understand if there is a problem and if so, how much, before we spend money on a problem we don't have.

You: One of our first steps after our first meeting with your team is to do a full audit and twelve months' use report. This will demonstrate the level of issues.

President: Have you talked to my head of operations or IT about this?

You: We wanted to gauge your interest before making a larger presentation.

President: Reach out to them and set some meeting times. I want to make certain that we understand what you are proposing and its impact. If we choose to work with you, how long from contract to implementation?

You: Aggressively, ninety days.

President: And how long until this breaks even?

You: It depends how long it takes to squeeze out the excess inventory from the system as well as set the right purchase triggers. Most of our customers see a breakeven within six months of implementation.

President: I can live with that. Let's schedule a call with our teams.

As you can see, even though it's one company being sold one solution, these are three very different conversations.

Throw out your existing scripts. You've got to get your head in the game and understand who you're talking to at each step of the way and what motivates them.

All the dynamics of positions and motivations come into play in the sales process. In the language of big sales, it is rarely one-size-fits-all messaging. You must focus your message on each person specifically by understanding where they are in the Layer Cake.

⭐ Key Takeaways

1. Every company has separate roles and job functions. For each of these positions, there are different motivations, effective terms, and ways in which they make purchase decisions. Knowing these differences will affect the language and approach used by sales professionals to present value (see page 93).

2. For each of the four positions discussed, there are five motivation categories: ambition, time scale, value concerns, buying concerns, and tenure (see page 98).

3. In a sales process, you may need to present to a buyer's table with different levels of the Layer Cake represented. You will need to be nimble in your presentation and communication to engage each of the buyers and influencers as your message is directed to each (see page 103).

4. Find more relevant resources at TheSecretToBigSales.com.

CHAPTER

6

Storytelling for Big Sales

Make your customer the hero of your sales story.

In the hit TV show *Mad Men*, a fictional accounting of the New York advertising world in the 1960s, lead adman Don Draper sells campaigns to his era's biggest companies. At some point in each of his presentations, Don tells a story that illustrates the explicit difference the advertisement would make in the consumer's purchasing behavior. The executives are always in awe, Don always gives a confident and somewhat smug smile, and the deal is done.

I always wondered if non-sales professionals watching the show could tell what was real and what was ridiculous. It's like asking doctors about medical shows or lawyers about legal shows—they'll mostly say, "What you see on those shows is complete B.S., that's not how it works." While some of the storylines and events were certainly contrived, I found the use of storytelling in sales particularly on point. I cannot overestimate the importance of creating a narrative as part of your selling solution.

Let's start off with a real-life example and then explore how it works and how you can make your own big sale story. Here is a story an ice cream producer gave to a national grocery chain executive:

> Successful grocery stores are measured by their revenue and margin per square foot. This means that the role of a national grocery chain leader is that of a real estate agent. They are paid to look at yield per square foot. They aren't necessarily worried about immaterial things like the flavor of the goods, the layout of the store, or the friendliness of the workers.

The difference that a grocery chain leader can make on their P&L occurs in less than 40% of the store. This is called "the donut." The donut is made up of all of the departments whose quality leadership can meaningfully improve: what it sells, the staff that helps stock and sell it, and the resulting margin. This usually includes the bakery, deli, butcher, fresh fruits, and vegetables—all of these departments are on the edge ring of the store's donut. The hole is filled with stuff they can't control—paper goods, canned goods, pet supplies, and everything else in the aisles—because these prices are dictated by the national distributors. This means there is little margin to be made or yield to increase.

There is, however, a portion of the store over which a grocery can increase both margin and yield—ice cream. The improvement comes from our aggressive pricing, high-quality product, and repeat purchases. The volume and frequency of these purchases justify the number of shelves used to display our flavors.

"I cannot overestimate the importance of creating a narrative as part of your selling solution"

We introduce and accelerate the purchase and repeat purchase of ice cream on a per store basis, and we do it in three ways:

1. We sell at a price $1 higher than any of the highest-priced brands.
2. We manage the digital as well as in-store marketing to drive buyers to our product.
3. We have created an unrepeatable quality to the ice cream that is preferred by customers.

The price drives the product's unique declared message: "This is the best tasting and highest value in the category, otherwise, how could it be sold at such a price?" This creates intrigue and first-time purchases.

Preference creates second purchases with multiple units purchased per grocery store visit. This increased number of units provides higher revenue and margin per shelf/square foot over the frozen food section.

The unique and historically successful approach to marketing this high-end dessert purchase creates speed to first purchase. First purchase is the key to sales growth for the introduction of a new product to a category in a store. If there is not a "pop" experience where the customer can try the product quickly, then first purchases take a long time. This means an expensive opportunity cost transition from the current product to our product.

We have chocolate chips—big and unique chocolate chips. Because our ice cream is made and packed by hand using the French-pot process, we can create our chips in-house. We are our own chocolatier. Our chips are made in such a way that no single unit of ice cream will have the same shape of chips. Our chips are as big as a thumb down to the size of a pencil eraser. Our chips are unique, delicious, and memorable. We make great ice cream, many manufacturers do. However, our unique chips create repeat purchases more quickly. The ice cream shelves become a higher revenue source because of price and a higher yield because of margin opportunities and driven marketing that leverages our unique chips, which have not been duplicated by any other ice cream manufacturer in over one hundred years of our company's history.

THE BUILDING BLOCKS

1. Knowing your audience

This story was told to the executives of store operations. The story was about the issues they deal with every day. The company could have talked about their ability to fulfill orders on time or their sustainable packaging, but they didn't. The reason being that the people who care about those things weren't there. The story was tailored to the audience—i.e., "my product will increase your per square foot yield."

2. Getting down on the ground

The story invokes "the frozen food section," and the "bakery, butcher, fresh fruits, and vegetables." The point of view is walking through the store and the challenges of running a store successfully. The pitch isn't some out-of-context array of slides and numbers, it's in the trenches.

3. Creating characters

The customers have personalities, they are shopping around the store looking for ice cream, they are caught off guard but intrigued by the price. They like the chocolate chips so much they come back for multiple pints. The audience can see and imagine these people shopping in their stores.

Similarly, the grocery chain leader in the story is frustrated that they can only control about 40% of their margin. The ice cream company swoops in to show there might be opportunity to up this percentage.

4. Offering the simple solution

Every significant solution has complexity to it. However, in a big sale, the early story should be told to establish the big picture. You do not tell the story of ice cream manufacturing from the perspective of a farmer or chef who has worked years on developing the recipe. This sort of nitty-gritty story comes much later. The first and most important stories tell why there is a problem or opportunity, what the impact is, and what it would mean to solve it.

5. Living happily ever after

"Memorable," "higher yield," and "speed to first purchase." The audience and their avatars, those characters in the story, need to be told the future of their "happily ever after." What does it feel like when the solution is implemented?

"Every significant solution has complexity to it. However, in a big sale, the early story should be told to establish the big picture"

⚠ Storytelling Traps to Avoid

1. "If it were me"

This is a classic salesperson conceit. "I know more about my prospect's business than they do, and if I were leading their company, this is how I would be running it." Obviously if you were running their company and selling to their company, you would buy your product. That's a no-brainer, which is to say there is no brain involved.

You can't say, "If I were in their shoes …" It's not productive. Don't put yourself in their shoes, figure them out in their shoes. Think from their perspective. Do the research for what the prospect thinks is their problem and then shift the lens to the problem you are going to solve.

2. "Should"

One of the challenges about being as informed as your prospect is the temptation to tell them what they should do. It takes a great deal of trust for senior executive buyers to listen to an outside voice telling them what they should do. Presenting options? Possible if you have demonstrated relevance and expertise. Telling them what to do? Not a great idea.

3. "Any questions so far?"

Do not seek cliché information. Don't stop talking and ask, "Any questions so far?" "Does this make sense?" "Is everyone on track and on the same page?" These are examples of false confirmations. If you are presenting a story, these types of confirmations are unnecessary and borderline rude.

4. "Let's take *you* for instance"

Don't put a specific audience member into the story. This isn't a magic trick. When you put a member of the presentation audience into the discussion as an active participant in your story, you have shifted the focus in the wrong direction. The person who has been selected will be uncomfortable and possibly insulted. The audience is no longer listening to your story or presentation, they are watching their co-worker and what happens to that person.

THE STORY CONSTRUCTION PROCESS

If you show prospects a packet of statistics and numbers, it might be somewhat interesting and helpful, but it won't be memorable. *That* is where storytelling comes in. You've got to give the people something they can remember easily, something they'll have no problem thinking about when they go home that night. Something they can replay in their heads in their own time. Stories last longer than data, and they make a bigger impact. Now that you understand the building blocks, you've got to understand the higher-level process that puts the blocks together.

1. Shift the Lens

In Hollywood, they say you can make a great script into a bad movie, but you can't make a bad script into a good movie. Similarly in sales, to tell a good story, you must actually have a good story. In the case of a big sale, underpinning your story with a unique take on a familiar problem will keep your audience's attention. The idea that 60% of the margin that the grocery chain leader thought was permanently frozen—pun intended—was actually able to be lessened was a completely unique perspective.

Find the angle from which you can look at the problem uniquely compared with competitors and even the buying team.

In one instance, an extruded rubber parts manufacturer liked to tour people through its plant to show what great parts they made. There was aerosol rubber everywhere, the space was a bit dark, the smell was awful, but they thought that's what buyers wanted to see! It wasn't working—until it was complemented by a story. Then, in one instance, the floor operations manager entered a prospect meeting. He had looked at the 64 SKUs that his company was bidding on, and with rubber underneath his fingernails and a dirty work shirt on his back, he said:

"These windshield wipers you have designed here are glued at the seams. If you ever drive in a rainstorm and the seams on the wipers split, it's because these weren't heat joined coming out of the production line. I have no idea how many returns you get on these, but I bet it's a lot. And I wanted to talk to you about SKU 9 as well. You have burrs in some of the grooves. They're tiny but they're a problem. You'll gum up the shielding. I'd throw these in the cryo-processor, freeze off all these burrs, and then finish wash them. You have a couple other parts that need to be either heat joined, reduce three components down to two, or cryo the excess. They're not all bad, I'm just saying that they could be made much better and last much longer."

"If you show prospects a packet of statistics and numbers, it might be somewhat interesting and helpful, but it won't be memorable. *That* is where storytelling comes in"

Just like that, his story shifted the lens from volume and price to quality and design. Once the lens was moved, the buyer shifted their business to his company.

2. Research the Future Path

The path is what takes your audience to its destination. You must look deeply at the other company's business, market, competitors, and customers so you can find the path to your own story. The path brings the audience to a new conclusion from a new perspective that allows your new view to work. To get this right, you must do a lot of research and that must be more about the prospect's challenges rather than your solutions.

I was speaking to a conference of medical device sales executives. I put up a timeline showing the past, a point of market inflection, and who the losers and winners would be after that point of inflection.

"In the past, your sales targets were surgeons. By educating them and persuading them to use your devices, you were able to develop relationships and become their device partner of choice. As a part of their surgeries, there were occasions when you might be in the operating bay during the surgery to provide expert insights. That is a very rewarding experience, but it's going away.

In the past two years and over the next three years, the hospital systems in the US will decrease from six thousand locations to four thousand. Consolidation because of costs and compliance will reduce hospital systems for larger cities to a national for-profit provider, an educational provider, and a faith-based hospital system. In many cities, there may be only two of those types of hospitals and care sites.

Over the same period, specialists including OB-GYN, cardiology groups, joint replacement, and other practices will be purchased by hospitals at the expected rate of 70% rather than only 20% today.

Why does this matter? Because surgeons are no longer your buyers, hospitals are. Part of their initial efforts as a hospital is the standardization of all elements of newly acquired practices. How long a procedure should take, what staff should be present, and the standardization of the tools and devices used is important to this group. When surgeons had the choice, there may have been a long list of possible device providers and treatment approaches. However, when the hospital standardizes, you will either be on the short list of device providers, or you will not have a customer because the surgeon no longer has the choice."

This same information was as available to anyone else in the room as it was to me. The difference was that I had walked the path into the future. My research gave me an insight that the attendees did not have.

3. Pick Your Villains and Heroes

Most good stories have a villain and a hero. In this last story, hospital consolidation and purchasing of specialist practices was the villain. In the story at the beginning of the chapter, the grocery store's donut and frozen margin was the villain. What you know about the villains creates the context for the heroic act that becomes the high point of your story.

My go-to villains tend to be outside of the prospect's control. Let's go over some of the most common culprits:

→ **Competitors**

This could be foreign providers or companies trying to buy market share by slashing prices below cost. Regardless, the competitors of your prospect are the ones you want to help them beat in the marketplace. Every company has a nemesis. Find out who their nemesis is and be the solution.

→ **Market**

Markets can swing rapidly from one favorite product to another. Internet apps go from hot to not in under forty-five days. Restaurants, movies, travel destinations, and other consumer-preferred purchases move all the time. The same is true for industrial or commercial markets. Technologies go in and out of favor. Integrated systems are changed out. Your prospect is fighting an ever-shifting marketplace and needs a provider that understands the challenges and can speak about them intelligently and provide solutions to be more resilient.

→ **Margin Compression**

Costs are going up and prices are going down. This is the recipe for margin compression. This is a constant business challenge for most of your prospect base. If you understand the unique challenges in your prospect's world, you can be the hero of their margin preservation story.

→ **Technology**

Often, leapfrogging technology is introduced that immediately jumps past the benefits your prospect has been developing and delivering. One of my friends had developed a flavor mixer that could create any fountain drink flavor with just six canisters of flavors. Not only that, but users could create their own flavors and they would be saved so that a user could go to their name on a screen and push a button to get their custom flavor. He had put tens of thousands of dollars into the design, programming, and prototype. He was setting his meetings with the major beverage manufacturers when Coca-Cola announced an all-in-one machine. Just like that, Coca-Cola's technology had leapt past my friend's approach. Your prospect may be facing a sea change in its industry that requires a better solution. Can you identify it and be their hero?

"What you know about the villains creates the context for the heroic act that becomes the high point of your story"

→ **Regulation**

Businesses face increasing regulation. Compliance, including quality control checks, documentation, and agency oversight, increases costs just for managing the burden. Add the costs of possible violations and the resulting potential for shutdowns and it is an enormous villain.

4. Be a Hero

At this point, you've helped your prospect see their challenges in a new way, you have walked the path with them, and you have pointed out the villains. It would be great if you could just raise your hands and yell, "Begone," but that only works in the wizard movies. To be the hero, you need to solve the problem behind the problem. That's the problem you uncovered when you shifted the lens. You can use your credibility and the understanding you have demonstrated in the presentation to build your solution.

As you can see, storytelling isn't just a good PowerPoint presentation. In fact, it shouldn't even include a presentation. A good story draws the buyer's team in and makes them see their problem and their solution in a new light. The only way to tell a great story is to have information your competitors don't have. The only way to get that information is to ask great questions, which we'll learn about in the next chapter.

⭐ Key Takeaways

1. Senior executive buyers want numbers but remember stories (see page 109).

2. There is a map to creating any sales presentation story (see page 111).

3. The building blocks of an effective sales story include knowing your audience, getting down on the ground, creating characters, offering the simple solution, and living happily ever after (see page 111).

4. Effective stories make changes in the minds of those who hear them. For that, you need to: shift the lens, research the future path, pick your villains and heroes, and be a hero (see page 115).

5. Find more relevant resources at TheSecretToBigSales.com.

CHAPTER

7

Great Question!

Ask great questions to get information you can leverage.

When you want to hunt and land big deals, the key to your success lies in the information you can get about your prospects. You can learn many facts about your prospect from a website, annual report, strategic plan, or RFP, but so can your competitors. To land big sales, what you need is depth of information, not only breadth. You need information that isn't readily available to the public. You need information that will help you match your prospect's problems to your solutions. The first set of questions I learned to ask was actually a list of things I should know about a prospect or customer. In Harvey Mackay's book *Swim with the Sharks without Being Eaten Alive*, he has a chapter called "The Mackay Customer Profile." It's a list of sixty-six questions you should be able to answer. This was back in 1988 and now you can get most of the answers to these questions online. But that's the point of this chapter. Many of your competitors are stuck with some version of the 1988 Mackay Sixty-Six Customer Profile. Your questions have to be much better because then your insight will be much better. You may already ask good questions, but you need to ask *great* questions.

Great questions have three advantages over merely *good* questions.

1. **They get the information you actually need.**

    This is no small thing. I often run into salespeople who are operating with so little information—usually due to asking suboptimal questions—that I can see right away they will not be able to land the deals they want. You shouldn't settle for the readily available information; it's up to you to ask the necessary questions. You need to anticipate all the problem areas, figure out the best questions to ask, and ask them.

An added bonus is that your competitors won't have the kinds of information you have.

2. They force the buyer to dig deep.
A well-worded question requires a well-thought-out answer. Depending on the exact words you use, your buyer must take the time to consider the implications of your question. In doing so, the buyer becomes part of your solution and helps you win their business without clearly realizing that's what they're doing.

3. They help you identify where you are in the process.
Great questions give you clues that are hard to discover any other way. For example, if the buyers give you general answers to your specific questions, they're probably not interested in doing the deal with you. If they are completely evasive or say they don't have the time, they aren't interested. But if they take the time to consider what you've asked and to give you a complete answer, they're probably interested in working with you.

"You may already ask good questions, but you need to ask *great* questions"

The truth is, good questions are often vague and result in vague answers. *Great* questions, on the other hand, are specific, historical, behavioral, narrative, and vulnerable. In the following pages, we'll look at each of these characteristics in more detail and we'll compare good vs. great questions so you can understand how to leverage your prospect's experience and knowledge to win big sales.

THE GENEALOGY OF A GREAT QUESTION

Great questions drive to the heart of an issue and ask for specific information. The more specific the question, the more specific the answer you will get. That's why when you ask anyone on the planet "How are you?" they will say, "Good, you?" even though the answer is usually much more complex than that. Vague questions beget vague answers.

Great questions ask for:

Historical Information: Past behavior is the best indicator of future behavior. Asking about specific circumstances from the past gives you a unique vision of how your prospect operates. When you ask a prospect what has happened in the past, they will frequently give you the context around the question. Understanding the context of a historical choice provides insight into how the prospect or their company makes a decision. A historical context question is, "What was going on in the company when you made the choice to buy from your current supplier?" The follow-up question is, "What has changed?" That provides a more complete response than "Why did you buy from your current supplier?"

Behavioral Information: We want to know what people have done or will do, not what their opinions are. That's why the great questions are specific and historical. They show real behavior by asking, "What have you learned from [insert event or choice here] that you are teaching your team?" Learning is the receipt of the data, but the teaching is what the behavioral response is. You want to ask questions that are answered by the behavioral response of the individual or the company. We'll review more examples later in this chapter.

Vulnerability: You'll want to learn about the authentic person in the conversation. For example, great questions let you learn who the real buyer is, who is most impacted by your solution, and who can do you the most harm, among other things. All the characteristics of great questions presented so far include some measure of vulnerability. The characteristic of a vulnerable question is to ask what opinion, excitement, or regret emerged because of what has happened or is happening. It steps past the intellectual and informational qualities and into the emotional characteristics. "How did the other person feel?" "How did you feel about how the business was, going into the pandemic?" "What is your sense of how the company's people are feeling since the introduction of the CRM system?" "What's the biggest concern of your team right now?"

> ### ❓ Questions You Should Ask Yourself
>
> When crafting great questions for your buyer, you're also answering a set of internal questions for you and your team. You need these questions answered, in your terms, in order to understand how to create a solution for your buyer. These questions might include the following:
>
> 1. Is this a real opportunity or a waste of time?
> 2. Who is the real decision maker?
> 3. Can we win if we are not the lowest priced?
> 4. Am I talking to the right people?
> 5. What will it take to win this business through my proposal?
>
> While it may seem counterintuitive, sometimes the best way to plan your strategy is to ask yourself, "How are we going to lose?" Often, salespeople will have the inclination to answer this question with confidence: "I don't see how they can't pick us." Or: "We've already got this deal, we just need a signature." However, strategy can be planned around the answers you come up with. These answers will provide new strategies or insights and inform what questions you need to ask of your buyer in order to give them a deal they won't refuse.

WHO, WHAT, AND WHERE, BUT NEVER WHY

There are some general rules to follow when asking questions:

- → Never be accusatory or personal.
- → Make your questions short and to the point.
- → Address only one topic per question.
- → Listen carefully and take notes as you get your answer.
- → Never ask questions that can be answered with a single word.

By this point in the chapter, these rules probably make sense at face value. But there is an unexpected final rule: Never ask a prospect "why?"

Asking "why," no matter the intention, often sounds challenging, attacking, and even indicting. The implication is that whatever event or course of action the prospect just recalled or proposed is crazy or stupid. Think of the last time you were asked, "Why did you do that?" Your immediate feeling was likely defensiveness. Answering would put you into a semi-hostile relationship with the questioner. Perhaps they were well-intentioned, only asking for information, but the implication of wrongheadedness is there, and you can feel it. The same will be true with your prospect.

If you understand *why* we ask why, you'll be able to come up with better ways of wording your inquiry such that it won't be perceived as hostile.

1. Understand Bad Decisions with Good Intentions

It's important to make your prospect feel validated that they made an intelligent decision at the time, even though it might be clear now to have been the wrong choice. This might look like the following questions:

→ "When you made the decision to go this route, what were the top one or two factors that brought you to this conclusion?"
→ "Weighing all of the information, it sounds like you had to make a difficult choice. What made the difference in choosing this solution?"
→ "In making this decision, there may have been a longer-term vision you were using in your selection. What were you aiming for in the long term?"

2. Determine Choices

Sometimes you want to know what choices your prospect had at the time that they made the questionable decision without telling them they made a dumb decision. These questions also ask for narrative responses that will provide a more expansive and helpful dialogue and give more context than just: *Why?*

→ "What would you have considered to be the riskier options at the time you selected this vendor?"
→ "You may have been considering other options when you made this choice. What was the second-best option in your mind at that time?"
→ "In making this decision, were there short-range, mid-range, and long-range alternatives? If so, into which category would you put this decision?"

3. Determine Circumstances

At other times you may be asking why because you want to better understand what greater circumstances were happening that led to the suboptimal decision. It's important to frame your question alongside the adage "If I had known better, I would have done better." Asking about circumstances in a respectful way also often can give you awareness of what the prospect is dealing with currently—i.e., how times have changed since the bad decision—and other insights into their motivations.

- → "What were the business initiatives driving this choice at the time it was made?"
- → "What has changed in your marketplace since this decision that would cause you to come to a different conclusion now?"
- → "What do you know now that you didn't know when you made your choice that would cause you to make a different choice?"

❓ Be Curious, Not Defensive

When challenged, it's best not to answer directly because you will seem defensive. Instead, be curious. Rather than addressing their statement directly, ask a question. Why did they challenge you? What led them to their current conclusion? How does their process work?

Buyer's team: I don't know if there is any reason we should go forward at this point.
Seller's team: Maybe not, but why did you agree to this meeting? What were you hoping we would end up with?

Buyer's team: This seems like a good solution. Let our team talk about it and we'll get back to you.
Seller's team: When you meet after a meeting like this one, if I can ask, what do you talk about?

Buyer's team: Honestly, what you are presenting is very similar to what we are doing already.
Seller's team: Often the devil's in the details. What specifics are different from or not similar to what you are doing?

"When challenged, it's best not to answer directly because you will seem defensive. Instead, be curious"

THE CATAPULT TOOL

Using the acronym CATAPULT, I created a tool that can help turn good questions into great questions. Basically, each letter stands for a word you should keep in mind when phrasing your questions. Each one softens the blow of any "why?" type questions, and ensures you get the specific information you need to close the deal. CATAPULT stands for:

- C → **CHANGE**
- A → **AFTER**
- T → **THRESHOLD**
- A → **ALWAYS/NEVER**
- P → **PROCESS**
- U → **UNDER WHAT CONDITIONS**
- L → **LEARN/TEACH**
- T → **TIME-BOUND**

The following are some examples of comparisons between good and great questions using the terms and words from CATAPULT to make changes.

C CHANGE

Adding the word "change" is just a nice and simple way of asking why.

Good: Why are you doing this project?
Great: What has <u>changed</u> in the past six months that is motivating this project?

Good: How has the economic downturn affected you?
Great: What things are you doing now that have <u>changed</u> over the past three years that are giving you a margin of advantage in the market?

Good: Is there much turnover among your vendors?
Great: Within the past two years, how many times have you <u>changed</u> vendors?

Good: How long is your selling process?
Great: How has your timeline for onboarding a new vendor <u>changed</u> in the past two years?

Good: What kinds of vendors are you hiring?
Great: How have the major characteristics, such as size, of your new vendors <u>changed</u> in the past year?

A AFTER

An "after" question emphasizes a specific event and the effect it had on the company or the effect the prospect believes it will have in the future. So, the questions might be historical and give you information about the past: "What did you do after X happened?" Or your question might be hypothetical: "What will happen after X takes place?"

Good: What's your vision for your company?
Great: In an ideal state, what will things look like <u>after</u> the transition to a new provider like us?

Good: What are your feelings about the future of this project?
Great: What ROI must you see <u>after</u> implementation of this project is complete to make it successful for you?

Good: Can you make these changes quickly?
Great: How long <u>after</u> contract signing will it take you to get your personnel changes made?

Good: How soon can you start on this project?
Great: What period is acceptable <u>after</u> contract signing for full implementation to begin?

T THRESHOLD

"Threshold" questions are great because they assume a closed deal by declaring the level of anticipated performance that needs to be achieved. If achieved, the shared assumption between the buyer's team and yours is that the work will come to you.

Good: What are your quality expectations?
Great: What performance <u>threshold</u> is necessary for you to justify the costs of bringing on a new provider?

Good: Are you satisfied with your logistics in delivering your product?
Great: How do you measure your current <u>threshold</u> of satisfaction across your supply chain at each step?

Good: What kind of financial return are you expecting?
Great: Is there a <u>threshold</u> of ROI that must be attained in justifying any project in your company, and if so, what is it?

A ALWAYS/NEVER

Absolute questions typically reveal past issues of failure. The answers can also present information about organizational guidelines, the guardrails that your solution needs to stay within to be acceptable.

Good: What do you look for in a new vendor?
Great: Based upon your experience, what do you <u>always</u> insist upon with a new vendor?

Good: What do you look for in a new vendor?
Great: What will you <u>never</u> tolerate with a new vendor?

Good: What are your selection criteria?
Great: Are there any selection criteria for you that are absolutes—meaning <u>always</u> present or <u>never</u> allowed?

🅿 PROCESS

Who questions are certainly better than *why* questions, but they often don't yield the information or response you were hoping for. I always say, if you want to get people answers, ask process questions. People often ask questions like:

→ "X seems to be against this project, how come?"
→ "Why can't I get any response to my questions from X?"
→ "Who has the final sign-off on this project?"

To these questions, you will either get an evasive answer, no answer, or an incorrect answer. It is better to ask process questions to determine who is making the choices and decisions and when.

Good: Who oversaw the selection of the vendor the last time you changed providers?
Great: What process did you use for selecting a new vendor the last time you changed providers?

Good: How do you decide which of your vendors to keep when you compare them?
Great: How does your company analyze the effectiveness of its vendor selection process?

Good: If I bring you a "mafia offer," what are my chances of winning this business?
Great: Does your company ever completely alter the buying process in order to take advantage of a wonderful opportunity?

U. UNDER WHAT CONDITIONS

This is often a question of last resort. You use this question when the buyer's table has shut your company down because they are unwilling to consider any choices but the ones that they have already made. However, there are always conditions under which a company will make a different decision.

Before the 1980 Olympics, Coca-Cola was negotiating its contract for advertising with the Olympic Committee and the networks. During a brainstorming session about the elements of the contract, a young person was delivering coffee and sandwiches to the room. The question that hung in the room was, "Are there any other contingencies we should put into the contract before we sign it? What's the worst thing that could happen?" Without thinking about it, the coffee guy said, "It would be terrible if you threw a party, and no one showed up."

A year or more later, President Jimmy Carter declared that the US would boycott the Russian-held Olympics. Because the clause was in the contract, Coca-Cola saved millions of advertising dollars.

...

Good: Is there anything we can do to change your mind?
Great: <u>Under what conditions</u> would you be willing to make a 100% change in providers?

...

Good: How do you know if the program worked or not?
Great: <u>Under what conditions</u> will you be able to declare this project/program a success?

...

Good: Are there people in your company who are looking for a solution like this?
Great: <u>Under what conditions</u> internally do you believe this change will have the greatest potential for success?

...

Good: Have we made any mistakes in this selling process?
Great: <u>Under what conditions</u> do companies trying to do business with your company usually trip themselves up?

L LEARN/TEACH

Leaders of buying teams have scars. They have probably made horrible decisions or watched subordinates make painfully bad decisions. The difference between education and learning is that learning hurts. When you ask these types of questions, you are focusing on the absolute pain point of their last purchase decision.

Good: How did your last provider replacement go?
Great: What did you <u>learn</u> the last time you changed providers that you are <u>teaching</u> your team now?

Good: What did your company do during the last economic downturn?
Great: What did your company <u>learn</u> during the last economic downturn as it relates to this decision that you are <u>teaching</u> all your people?

Good: What is the one thing you wish every one of your vendors understood?
Great: What is the biggest lesson you'd like to <u>teach</u> prospective vendors so they could be successful in doing business with you?

Good: How did your last successful rollout go for your new technology?
Great: What was the last successful company-wide rollout of a new solution and what did your team <u>learn</u>?

T TIME-BOUND

Memories are murky. When you ask a question about your prospect's perspective, it must be defined to a window of time. Otherwise, your answers will be about generalities and not changes. Changes show where your opportunities are.

Good: Why are you considering new partners now?
Great: In the <u>past six months</u>, what has changed that makes it the right <u>time</u> to consider a new partner?

Good: What are the issues you are concerned with?
Great: <u>Since the merger</u>, what have been the biggest challenges in this area that you and your team have faced?

Good: How do you think your company is regarding its compliance?
Great: With the <u>passing of the new regulation</u>, what impact will this project have on your overall compliance requirements?

I went with a client's sales professional to a sales call with a multinational consumer goods corporation worth over $100 billion. I was there to observe and provide feedback as he was selling specialized marketing services. We were meeting with who we thought was the senior executive buyer and her assistant director. The sales professional began to talk about his company, their history, and why it would be a good partner. I interjected while everyone was talking:

Question 1: "I'm sorry, I need to interrupt. Why are you here? Why did you agree to see us?"
Senior Executive Buyer: "We were excited about what we heard from the phone call, and we wanted to hear what you had to say."

Question 2: "Great. What problem is it that you are hoping we can help with?"
Senior Executive Buyer: "We like to look at different marketing approaches to keep current with the marketplace and then determine if a pilot is a good idea."

Question 3: "How do you know if a pilot makes sense? What sort of rubric or performance threshold do you use?"
Senior Executive Buyer: "It depends on the problem and which of our products or divisions can use the service. We use our company's agency to review the approach and manage the pilot."

Question 4: "For the sake of a better understanding of how we can serve you best, can you walk me through the process of qualifying for a pilot, evaluating the results, and then implementing the services of a company like ours?"

Using the CATAPULT tool, I was able to infer that this deal was not going to happen in four simple questions. Question 3, for example, is the first T in CATAPULT, threshold. I wanted to know what they were looking to see in a successful pilot. Next, because their answer was too vague for my tastes, I asked a process question, the P in CATAPULT. I wanted to know what I could expect working on a pilot with them to look like.

> **"The right questions provide the information to determine whether you are in the right place talking to the right people about the right issues"**

Through the balance of the conversation, we learned that the overall process of achieving a contract of a measurable size for a marketing services company would happen over nineteen months and there would be twenty-four people involved in the buying process. This was their process, regardless of what we were selling. We said thank you and left.

Why? Because it would take nineteen months and millions of dollars on our part to learn that we might lose. Using the information-gathering questions featured in this chapter and also in Chapter 4 on identifying senior executive buyers, we were able to see the deal had no legs for us:

- → What is the performance threshold for a significant purchase? They could not say.
- → What problem would we be solving? They did not know.
- → How quickly did they need to solve the problem? No urgency if there is no problem.
- → Who was the senior executive buyer? They were not certain who the senior executive buyer might be.

This meeting was actually part of a market scan of intellectual property and marketing best practices, not a buying process.

Most sales professionals are thrilled to secure a meeting with an executive from a massive company. The belief here is that a sales professional must start somewhere and if they can just get in the door then good things can happen.

This is not the case when it comes to big sales. The right questions provide the information to determine whether you are in the right place talking to the right people about the right issues.

⭐ Key Takeaways

1. Be very careful when and how you ask the question "Why?" (see page 126).

2. There are key terms that can turn good questions into great questions (see page 130).

3. The system for creating great questions is the CATAPULT system (see page 130).

4. Find more relevant resources at TheSecretToBigSales.com.

Conclusion

This book is a toolkit for selling to senior executive buyers. Selling to senior executive buyers requires you to prompt them in their terms so you can respond in their terms. Using the language they use not only communicates to them that you're an expert, but it actually helps you see the world and their industry through their eyes. It helps you provide better solutions rather than whatever cookie-cutter solution you're used to offering.

Below, you'll find a conversation I had with a top-five bank credit issuer. You'll also find numerous references to the various parts of this book that explain what is happening in this conversation and why.

THE FIVE MOTIVATIONS, PAGE 98 ★

Me: "At a very high level, how do you make money from your credit cards?"
Prospect: "We make money off interest just like any other credit card."
Me: "When do you start making the interest money and on average how much per card?"
Prospect: "As long as they are carrying a balance, we are charging interest on the card, after the first thirty days, not before."

ANALYSIS, PAGE 47 ★

Me: "So, if they pay off their balance within thirty days, you do not generate any revenue."
Prospect: "Right."

THE PIVOT POINT, PAGE 52 ★

Me: "Up until now, we have been talking about how my company could help you get new customers. But it sounds like you lose money on customers until they have left balances on their cards for more than thirty days. So really you need balances longer than thirty days more than you need credit cards, right?"
Prospect: "Right. That's why we want more customers."

> **THE CATAPULT TOOL, PAGE 130** ★

Me: "But what's the threshold where this makes sense? How much interest does it take to cover the initial cost of me adding the new credit cardholder?"
Prospect: "It depends on interest rate, amount charged, and how long the balance is not paid off."

> **NAPKIN MATH, PAGE 22** ★

Me: "On average, napkin math, what do you think?"
Prospect: "Using all of our marketing and sales channels, average is about $150 of interest paid by the customer to cover the cost of getting the customer."
Me: "For my company to be of value to you, we need to bring you customers who pay $150+ of interest within a year. We can do that by increasing the amount of money that is on the card and adding customers who are willing to pay a higher rate, and regardless, the balance is better if it remains on the card longer than thirty days."
Prospect: "You got it."

> **SHIFT THE LENS, PAGE 115** ★

Me: "My company is therefore proposing that you pay us on balances rather than issued cards. By using our data filtering tools, a proprietary system for making customer contacts more efficient, and bringing customers to the bank who are already carrying a balance, we increase the likelihood that your new credit cardholders will generate more interest. In other words, if your previous stated goal was 1,000,000 new credit cardholders generating a minimum of $150 in interest, then the goal is to achieve $150 million in interest from new credit cardholders. If we do this more efficiently than your $150 million annual interest, you win. It's less expensive than hiring me to add 1,000,000 new cardholders to achieve the same benefit of the $150 million in interest. If I can do both, generate the 1,000,000 new cardholders and each is carrying an interest-generating balance of greater than $150 per year, you win again."

This conversation succinctly shows how language can be used to land big sales:

→ It started and ended with money as the true result to measure.
→ It demonstrated a clear understanding of the prospect's industry in plain language.

- → It changed the way in which the buyer was considering their options. Our competitors wanted to add credit cardholders. We wanted to add interest-bearing balances.
- → It discerned the price the buyer was willing to pay for a new credit cardholder, $150 per customer, without directly asking the price the buyer was willing to pay.

It was time-bound by declaration of one year to be the increment of benefit.

As this book comes to a close, I hope you see now that these ideas do not require you to be flashy or make a better presentation, nor even make a pitch at all. They ask for you to improve your conversations—whether they be in meetings or presentations or through quick phone calls—to meaningfully connect with senior executives by using language they understand and that makes them feel understood. If you do this, you will increase your success and land big sales.

Other books by Tom Searcy and Carajane Moore

- How to Close a Deal Like Warren Buffett: Lessons from the World's Greatest Dealmaker — Tom Searcy and Henry DeVries
- How to Sell in Place: Closing Deals in the New Normal — Carajane Moore & Tom Searcy
- Life After the Death of Selling: How to Thrive in the New Era of Sales — Tom Searcy and Carajane Moore
- RFPs Suck! How to Master the RFP System Once and for All to Win Big Business — Tom Searcy
- The Secret to Big Sales: Use Executive Language to Close More Deals — Tom Searcy with Carajane Moore
- Whale Hunting: Land Big Sales and Transform Your Company — Tom Searcy and Barbara Weaver Smith

Acknowledgments

We would like to thank our families, friends, and raving fans, who inspire us to be our best and serve well every day. In addition, we would like to thank Josh Raab and his book production team at Raab & Co.—including Andrew Bell, Amélie Cherlin, and Reina Strauss—for their amazing insight, guidance, and patience through the editing and publishing process. Lastly, we would like to thank Nate Brooking, who is the rudder to our sails in keeping everything running in the right direction for the business.

Made in the USA
Monee, IL
13 September 2023

fb77a18e-7f25-4ffa-8aaa-08a3e3d621c8R01